Preparation and presentation of
the show dog
The complete handling guide

by JEFF and BETTY BRUCKER

Third Edition

Alpine
PUBLICATIONS
Loveland, Colorado

This book is available at special quantity discounts for breeders and for club promotions, premiums, or educational use. Write for details.

1 2 3 4 5 6 7 8 9 0

Printed in the United States of America.

Library of Congress Cataloging-in-Publication Data

Brucker, Jeff.
   Show dogs : preparation and presentation of the show dog : the complete handling guide / by Jeff and Betty Brucker ; compiled and edited by William W. Denlinger and R. Annabel Rathman.
     p. cm.
  Originally published : 3rd ed. Fairfax, VA. : Denlinger's Publishers, 1982.
  ISBN 0-931866-80-4 (pbk.)
  1. Dogs--Showing. 2. Show dogs.   I. Brucker, Betty.
II. Denlinger, William Watson, 1924-   . III. Rathman, R.
Annabel.   IV. Title.
SF425.B75   1995
636.7'0888--dc20   95-44723
                                            CIP

This book is dedicated to all of the dog show enthusiasts who give their time, energy, and devotion to the ongoing advancement of pure-bred dogs.

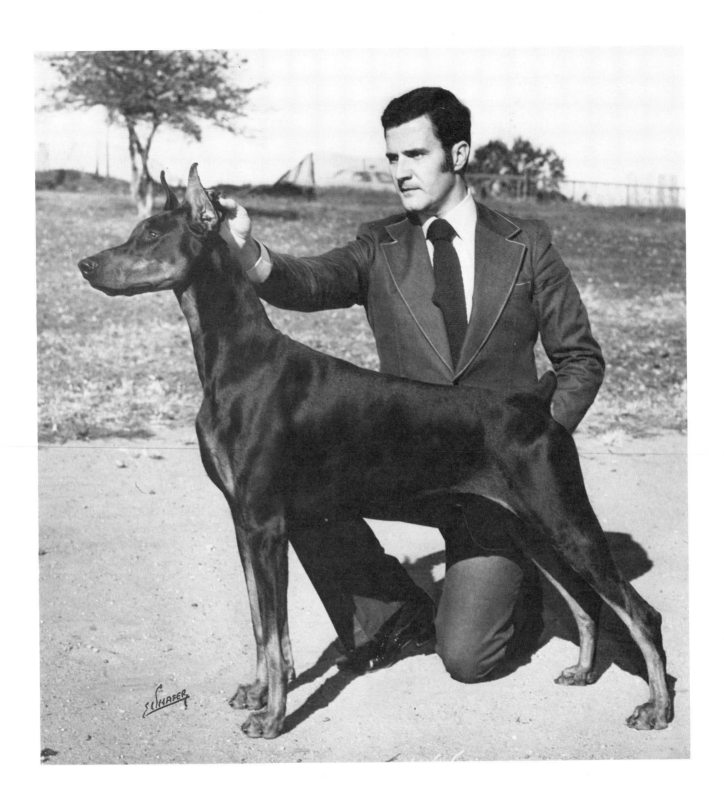

Foreword

Brucker Enterprises is dedicated to the belief that sportsmanship, courtesy, and professionalism will bring about a healthier and more enjoyable atmosphere in the dog show community. It is toward this aim that this book has been written—*Preparation and Presentation of the Show Dog—A Complete Handling Guide.*

Spanning a combined show ring experience of some thirty years, producing Best-in-Show wins from all Groups, and having trained more than twenty-five hundred people in the art of handling the show dog, we have tried to provide the dog show world and the general public with the benefit of our knowledge and experience. We feel that with an enthusiastic and sincere approach to learning about showing dogs, you the reader can expand your knowledge of the sport of showing dogs.

In closing, Brucker Enterprises adheres to and promotes its theme—*Sportsmanship Through Understanding*—and continues to strive for the improvement and advancement of purebred dog shows and the art of handling.

Jeffrey Brucker
Betty Brucker

CREDITS

Photographer of illustrative photos:
Bernard Kernan
Hackettstown, New Jersey

Permission of reprints:
American Kennel Club
New York City

Production Assistant:
Sidney Lynn
Huntington, New York

Friend:
Ray Carlisle
Spring Valley, New York

Photography:
Jeff Joffe
Miami, Florida

Illustrator:
Alden Cole
New York City

Table of Contents

1
World of Show Dogs

Exhibiting purebred dogs is one of the oldest sports in the United States. The first dog show was held about 1875 with a total entry in the low thirties. The following one hundred plus years have seen many changes in dog shows. Currently, some eight hundred all-breed shows and more than a thousand specialty shows are held each year in the United States, as well as some fifty-two hundred informal conformation matches and obedience trials.

The sport of exhibiting purebred dogs is a fast-growing and extremely popular one. For this many people to be actively involved in showing dogs, a great deal of satisfaction and enjoyment must be experienced by the participants. As with any competitive situation, much of the pleasure associated with the showing of a dog is the accomplishment derived from winning.

Winning can be interpreted differently by dog show participants, whether they are active or non-active in the actual showing process. To some, no less than the Best-in-Show selection can be considered success. To others, a Group placement or having their dog selected as Best of Breed is termed winning. The Winners Dog or Winners Bitch selection, or placement in one of the various classes means winning to others.

However one interprets the term, the fact remains that winning is still dependent upon many factors. Actually, the dog, the person handling the dog, and the judge will be in the ring. But consider all of the factors involved at a dog show and you can realize what is necessary to be successful in the world of show dogs. For example— selecting the right type and quality of dog, show training your dog, conditioning, grooming, making entries, handling the dog in the ring or contracting a professional handler, following judging results and keeping accurate records—to name only a few.

Hopefully, the dog is of a breed which is suitable to and compatible with the owners and their living environment. In all cases the dog should be the best possible representative of that breed. Referring to the breed Standards is necessary to achieve both of the above. Also, obtaining assistance is advisable. A professional handler, an experienced and successful exhibitor, or an ethical breeder is the best source of aid in the selection process. When in the ring, the dog must be well trained in order to perform the procedures necessary for breed competition.

At the other end of the lead, more things are involved. The person exhibiting the dog must be knowledgeable of dog shows in general and of ring procedure, decorum, etiquette, and judging procedure in particular. In addition, he must be very familiar with his dog, both the good aspects and the less desirable points. The handler of the dog is responsible for presenting the dog in the best manner possible, so if you feel that you cannot handle your dog yourself, seek out a professional.

The condition of the show ground can affect a dog's performance greatly. The weather can also play a part in the outcome of the show.

The most important factor is the judging of the dog. This is accomplished by the judge, who evaluates your dog against the Standard for that breed and then in comparison to the other dogs present in the ring on a particular day. In most cases, winning points and Best of Breed, not to mention Group placements and being selected Best in Show, are sporadic occurrences.

To improve your winning average, there are many things that can be done. This book will provide and explain the techniques and knowledge necessary to produce a thorough, consistent, and professional exhibition and presentation of your dog in the show ring.

10

2
Essential Show Training

Show training will be necessary for both you and your dog. The handling of a dog is by no means an easy task. In fact, what you need to know to show your dog can fill a whole book!

The first step in handling or training your show dog is to learn the basics. How skilled you become will depend upon your natural ability in handling dogs, how well you can assimilate the information, and how hard you are willing to work at it.

TRAINING YOURSELF

Attending shows and watching your breed in the ring will provide an excellent start. You will begin to notice who is doing a good job of showing their dog, based on how well the dog performs. Observe how dogs are stacked and baited, and the means used to gain and keep the attention of the dog.

Handling classes and seminars can be invaluable aids to your show training. Such courses usually are sponsored by breed clubs, with experienced professional handlers or knowledgeable exhibitors as instructors. The fee usually is nominal in relation to the hours of instruction and the value of the course. Hopefully, these classes and seminars will aid you in acquiring the skills needed to exhibit your dog and help you gain poise and confidence in the ring.

After you have acquired a few handling skills, but do not yet feel confident enough to enter point shows, match shows are an intermediate step. At a match, the routine is similar to that at a point show in pace, division of classes, and procedure, but a match does not give the exhibitor a hectic, overly competitive feeling. After you have shown in a few match shows, you should become more relaxed and knowledgeable, and be ready for point show competition.

TRAINING YOUR DOG

Regardless of when you obtain your dog, if he is going to be a show dog, training must begin immediately. Hopefully, he will be from a show home and much of the basic training will have been done. When working with any dog, regardless of age, there are several important factors to consider in training him. First, you must always be consistent. Be consistent in your expectations of the dog in general, in your training sessions, in praising him, and even in the correction you will have to give from time to time. Second, be realistic in the length of time you spend working with your dog, training him for the show ring. Ten or fifteen minutes at one session is the maximum time to work with a dog. If you or the dog become frustrated during a training session, stop immediately, and resume later.

Following are the essential components in training your dog to be a well-adjusted show dog.

Before showing your dog, one of the first steps needed is to learn the basics of handling. These people are attending a handling seminar where they are receiving instructions as well as "in the ring" experience in learning to show their own dog.

LEADBREAKING

Begin letting your dog get used to a collar by letting him walk around the house or in a confined area wearing one. To a puppy of seven or eight weeks, the weight of the collar seems heavy, and many dogs need a few days to adjust to the feeling of something around the neck. Next, attach a lead to the collar and allow the dog to walk where he pleases with you following along. When the dog is comfortable with the feeling of the lead and collar, he must be taught the correct way to walk on lead. With the dog always on your left side, let the collar hand loosely and with verbal encouragement and short tugs on the lead, try to keep your dog walking. If he stops, start the procedure over again, being calm and patient. This method of teaching your dog to walk on lead is more time-consuming than forcing him to submit, but will result in your having a happy dog, anxious to please. At the beginning, you may have to coax the dog along consistently by rubbing under his chin or throwing a ball for him to follow. You can be certain to meet with resistance. Continue lead training for five minutes, not more than two times per day, until the dog begins moving easily on lead. Then take short pleasure walks so that the dog will begin enjoying his time on lead.

Watching the professional handler in the ring is another excellent way to train yourself. Observe the procedures used by a professional handler in the ring while exhibiting his dog. Practice some of these techniques when working with your own dog.

SHOW ROUTINE

Getting your dog accustomed to the typical routine you will follow at shows can be helpful. First of all, he will need to become accustomed to riding in a vehicle. Many dogs suffer from motion sickness, which can make the day of a show a disaster. Taking your dog on short trips and being careful not to feed him for six hours before travelling will help his travelling behavior. Because you will probably use a crate at the show, you should acquaint your dog with it at home if you have not already done so. If your dog eats in his crate at home, then he will eat in his crate in any location—dog show, car, hotel room, etc. A dog that has a full fenced yard in which to take care of the necessary bathroom functions may refuse to do so in an exercise pen set up for him at the show site. At home, alternate the use of an exercise pen with the free run of the yard in order to assist your dog in learning what is expected of him. Many dogs will make themselves uncomfortable rather than perform their bathroom functions.

BEST OF
WINNERS
GREATER GAINESVILLE
DOG FANCIERS ASSN.
APRIL 1979
PHOTO BY BONNIE

SOCIALIZATION

In order for your show dog to have a healthy attitude toward people, it is necessary that he be socialized. Shopping malls are excellent places for your dog to be around a lot of people. Let people pet your dog and play with him a long as they are gentle with him.

Do not encourage your dog to rely on you all of the time and to become too dependent upon you. An overly dependent dog may sometimes develop temperament problems, such as shyness or nervousness, even when away from the owner for only a short period of time. Therefore, it is advisable that several members of the family be responsible for feeding, exercising, and training.

CORRECTION AND ATTENTION SOUNDS

Correction and attention sounds are two we have used successfully over the years. They become particularly important if the dog lives with you and if you handle him in the ring. Attention noises often are unsolicited, so when the animal shows attention to a car door closing or any unusual sound, go along with his enthusiasm. Make comments such as "What do you see?" or "What is it?" If you react several times in a consistent manner you soon will be able to bring on this excited, interested state merely by repeating the phrase. This is very desirable as a tactic for use in the show ring to encourage your dog to show animation and a positive attitude.

The same holds true for correction sounds. Decide on a sound to use whenever your dog does something wrong, then stop him and correct him while using this sound. Oftentimes the use of this sound alone will be enough to stop any undesirable action he might attempt. The ring is no place to display undesirable behavior.

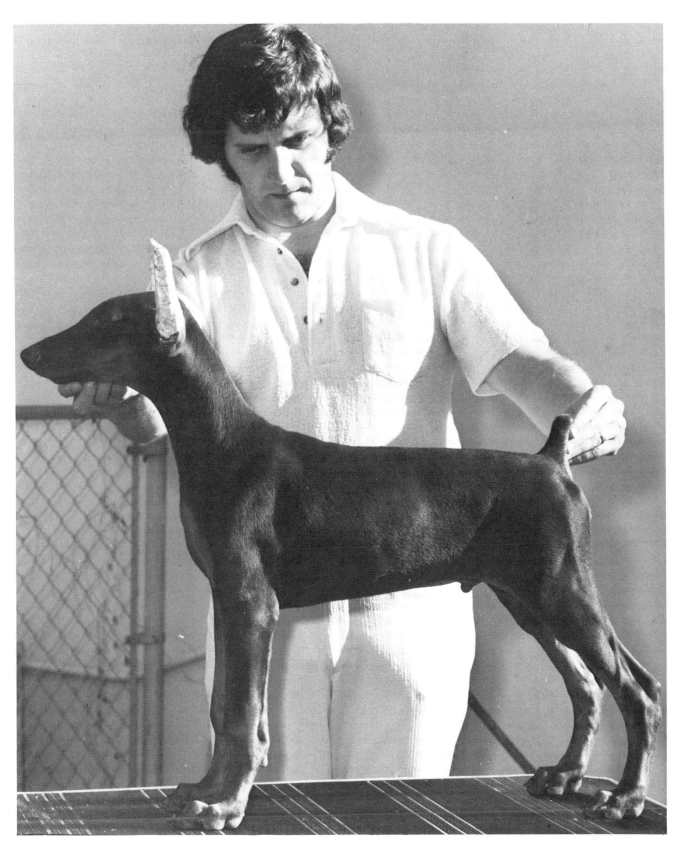

It is never too early to begin table training your dog. Be sure to select a firm and steady table with a non-skid surface. This young Doberman is well acquainted with the grooming table.

To teach your dog to lean forward and improve his natural stance, place the rear feet as far back on the table as possible.

in the same position. In the early stages of stacking, it is beneficial for the dog to feel someone examining him as a judge would do. He should be comfortable with having his mouth examined, and in the case of a male, also his testicles.

To teach your dog to lean forward and improve his stance, place his back feet as far back on the edge of the table as possible. Place one hand between the hind legs while putting the other hand under his chin to steady him. Push him slowly backwards, allowing his hind legs to fall off the table. But remember to keep a firm grip so as not to allow your puppy to hurt himself. And, of course, never allow him to fall. After putting his legs back on the table, be sure to praise your dog, for he must always relate training periods with fun. You may repeat this step two or three times per day.

TABLE TRAINING

A grooming table or other waist-high table with a firm non-skid surface is invaluable in training your dog. It is much easier for you to begin stacking your dog here, as a young puppy, rather than on the ground, although that is important also. The table is also the place for grooming to be done, for it is much easier for you to deal with your dog at this height. Never leave your dog alone on the table because he may jump off and injure himself.

To begin stacking your puppy on the grooming table, pose him as described in the section on stacking. In the beginning stages, it is more important that he keep his feet in position than that the stacked position be absolutely perfect. If he moves his foot, firmly replace it

Hold your dog under the chin and place your other hand near the rear area. Push him slowly backwards until his legs begin to fall off the table.

Keep a firm grip on your dog so as to not allow him to hurt himself. Under all circumstances, take precautions to avoid letting him fall.

Replace his back feet on the table. Repeat this procedure a few times each day. This will result in your dog's beginning to lean forward, whether on the grooming table or on the ground. It is advisable to begin this procedure as early as possible in your dog's life because some breeds mature quickly and are soon too large to be trained successfully using this procedure.

Under the dog's jaw is a "V" which is sometimes referred to as the *handle*.

3
Stacking Your Dog

The procedure of *stacking* refers to posing or positioning of your dog in the ring. Stacking is often termed "setting up," and serves the purpose of providing the judge with a proper view of your dog. A properly stacked show dog can display its conformation qualities to its best advantage. It is important to stack your dog correctly so that its outstanding features can be displayed to their maximum and at the same time faults can be minimized.

Here is the sequence of the basic steps you need to follow to stack your dog.

SETTING UP THE FRONT END

The dog should always be on your left side (except when the judge may be viewing your dog from the opposite side and, of course, you will never want to block his view). Practice walking your dog into a straight position because this will aid you in speeding up the stacking of your dog. If you must pull his body into line, this adds another step and time is always limited.

Step I—After halting your dog in a straight position, move the collar to the top of the neck, right behind the ear. Gather the lead into your right hand and place the tips of the fingers of your left hand in the "v" of the dog's lower jaw, often referred to as the handle. Transfer the lead to your left hand.

19

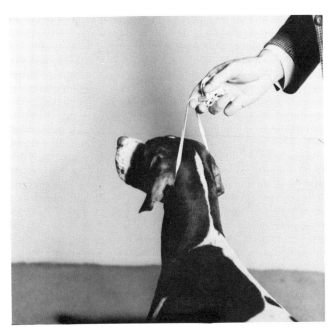

Step II—Place your right hand on the dog's right front elbow (while simultaneously lifting the head up and away with the left hand), placing the right foot to the ground squarely under the dog's right shoulder. The lead should remain gathered in the left hand while performing this step.

Step III—Transfer the gathered lead from the left hand to right, place your right hand under the jaw and pull the head upward and toward your body while grasping the left elbow with the left hand, placing that foot to the ground squarely under the dog's shoulder. Remember, always pull the head away from the leg you are placing.

Step IV—Now with the lead in the right hand, move the collar up and under the ears and pull upward with the lead still gathered.

Step V—Place the left hand at the base of the ears (or back of the neck) and adjust them so they are consistent with your breed Standard. Continue to hold the lead with the right hand.

Some breeds are stacked without the use of a lead or collar. Instead, the hand is used to steady and hold the head by grasping the "v" at the dog's lower jaw (handle), with the rest of the hand grasping the dog's muzzle.

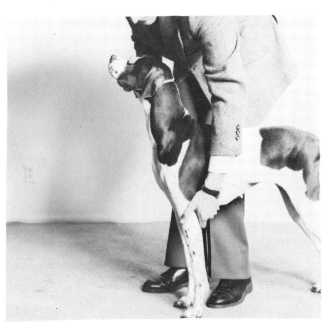

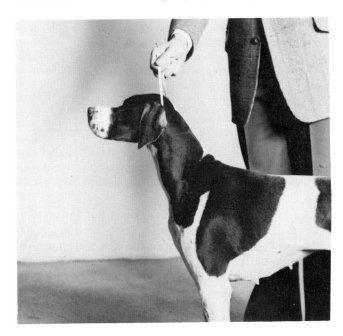

STACKING THE REAR QUARTERS

Step VI—In order to calm and prepare your dog to have its hindquarters stacked smoothly, it is important to have the collar and lead in the right hand and to move the left hand across the topline or side of the dog. Often, stroking the dog in this manner and adding a few calmly spoken words will serve to relax and steady the dog.

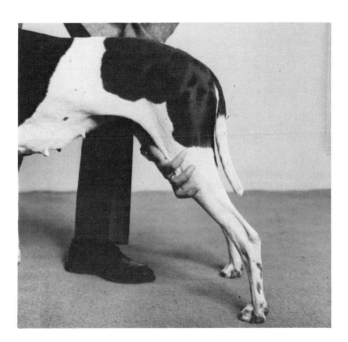

Step VIII—Reach under the loin of the dog and grasp the left hind leg in the mid-section and place the left paw squarely on the ground behind the rear of the dog. This hock should also be perpendicular with the ground. This paw should also be outside of the front paw position and should be the same distance back as the right rear paw. (This is the correct way of stacking all breeds except the German Shepherd Dog.)

Step VII—With the left hand, grasp the mid-portion of the right hind leg and place the right rear paw to the ground, extended squarely behind the rear. In placing the rear paw to the ground, the hock should be perpendicular to the ground. The rear paw should be placed approximately one inch outside of the front paw position.

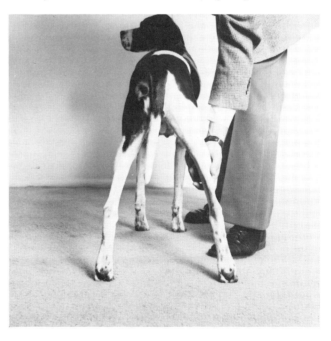

POSITIONING THE TAIL

The position of the tail varies from breed to breed. For the breeds that should have the tail elevated, rubbing under the tail often helps to encourage the dog to raise it to the proper position.

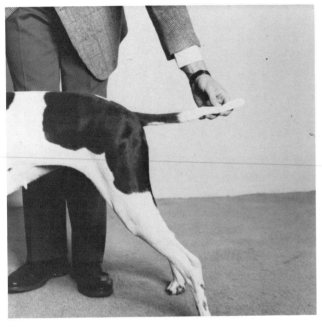

For this breed, the tail should be extended straight out from the body. The handler of the dog should hold the tail in the position that is correct for the breed.

The results of the steps of stacking are clearly evident in this photo of a perfectly posed dog. Remember to recheck the stacked position after you have completed all necessary steps once.

22

Some breeds should hold the tail erect but often do not!

Rubbing under the tail is often necessary to help achieve the correct tail carriage.

Push the tail up and continue to rub upward at the base of the tail.

Keep repeating this procedure until the dog begins to hold his tail correctly without assistance.

IMPROVING THE STACKED POSITION

It is always necessary after completing the above steps to check the dog quickly and reposition him if a foot has moved or the lead has slipped. This is especially important for the young or untrained dog.

To show length of neck and improve the topline, pull the head forward with your hands placed on either side of the ears. If the topline sags, and this is incorrect for the breed, place your hand under the stomach and push upward. For a dog that pulls back, sometimes referred to as *bridging* (refer also to the chapter on Show Training), place your hand under the tail and push forward to keep the dog in the correct position.

Having one hand holding the head and the other positioned near the rear is the best way to calm and steady the dog when it is being examined by the judge.

Some breeds can also be stacked without a lead. Without using the lead, set up the dog the same way that you would with a lead.

Showing the dog in a stacked position without a lead is an impressive sight and is usually reserved for those times when the judge is looking directly at your dog. Don't overuse this technique! Keep the lead close at hand in case you are asked to move or gait your dog.

In the case of a well trained and stable dog, you can move your hand away, allowing the dog to stand alone.

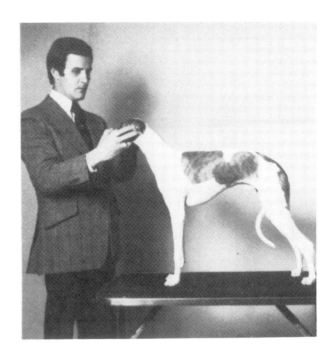

To show length of neck, grasp the head in both hands and pull upward from the base of the ears.

For a dog that pulls back, sometimes called *bridging*, hold the head firmly and push forward from the rear section near the tail.

Arch of neck can be accentuated by pulling up on the collar and pushing the front portion of the muzzle downward.

EXAMINATION BY JUDGE

It is important that the judge have as little trouble as possible when examining your dog. To accomplish this, follow these guidelines:

1. Keep your dog steady. To do this put one hand behind the neck at the back of the head to keep your dog from pulling its head away while the judge is examining the head.

2. The dog's mouth will need to be examined. The judge may examine the mouth himself or in some cases ask you to show the mouth. When you are showing the mouth, be sure to pull the lips all the way back to show the bite, and the number of teeth on each side, and then open the mouth. Remember the judge is the one who should be viewing the mouth, so keep your head and hands out of the way.

3. In the case of a male, the judge will need to examine the testicles. Following the same procedure as used when setting up the rear, have the collar in the right hand, steadying the head, and stroke the dog down the back with your left hand. Then place your left hand under the stomach while the judge examines the hindquarters and testicles.

Show the bite of your dog by pulling up the front lips, or flaps, of the dog. Remember to keep *your* head back and out of the judge's vision.

Pull the lips, or flaps, back on each side of the mouth. Keep your fingers out of the judge's view of the mouth.

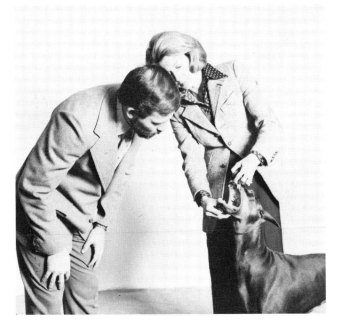

Open the mouth wide so that the judge is able to see all the way back in the mouth.

While the dog is being examined by the judge keep the dog steady. Place one hand behind the neck at the back of the head near the ears to keep your dog from pulling away while his front quarters are being examined.

Running your hand down the dog's back and side while the judge is examining him is another means of calming and steadying your dog. Be careful not to get your hands in the way of judge's examination.

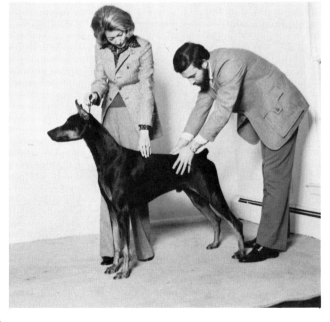

28

In the case of a male, move your hand under the dog's stomach when his testicles are examined.

When the judge begins to examine the rear of your dog, move your hand to the rear of the dog for the purpose of steadying the dog.

Maintain a reasonable distance away from other handlers and dogs when moving your dog around the ring. Keep your free arm tucked in toward your body. Be sure you are taking long, low strides close to the ground.

Practice moving around the ring without including your dog. First learn all the basics of good ring movement and ring patterns. Then practice them with a dog in hand.

Do not forget to keep glancing at the judge in case further instructions are given. Be aware of where the judge is standing at all times.

4
Movement

Moving your dog is an integral part of the "in the ring" procedure. Therefore, it is important to be aware of the basics of movement in order to exhibit your dog properly. In most breeds, desired movement is described specifically in the breed Standard. This further emphasizes the importance of displaying the dog's movement properly.

In the ring, you must follow certain guidelines in order to present the dog's movement to the judge properly. The judge will instruct you as to the pattern he would like you to follow. Before you start moving, be sure you are collected and are set to go. Make eye contact with the judge and be sure you have received a signal from the judge that he is ready to watch you make your pattern. If you are not first in line to make the pattern, it is important that you pay close attention to the instructions the judge gave to the others in the ring so that you will not make a mistake in your pattern.

In order that the judge may have a full view of the dog and its qualities of gait, the handler must remain as inconspicuous as possible, yet retain full control of the dog. To accomplish this, always run in a straight line with your dog, being sure that you take long low strides. Angling your body in toward your dog and bending slightly forward will improve your movement and enable you to glance quickly back over your left shoulder at the judge. Anticipate any turns or angles you may have to make,

and execute them clearly to keep your dog on an even route so as not to break gait.

If your coat or other clothing is flapping about, hair is flying, coins in the pocket are jangling, and the free arm is swinging wildly up and down, the judge cannot help but be distracted from watching the dog's movement. We will discuss proper dress and ring attire elsewhere, but if you wear a coat, be certain to button it. Remove change and keys from your pocket, and always make a conscious effort to hold your free arm tucked closely in toward your body. Not only does a swinging arm distract the judge, but it may distract the dog as well. If your right hand has held bait and the dog can still smell the aroma, his head will tend to follow the smell and if the hand moves, so will his head.

If you are holding your arm close to your body and are having a problem with your dog's looking up at you too much or not moving ahead properly, you might try pretending to toss a tiny bit of bait forward. This is accomplished by training your dog at home, where you will actually be using and throwing bait. To do this, take a small piece of bait and, as you are moving, throw it in the direction you are heading. Throw as far ahead and as smoothly as you can, then quickly pull your hand back in close to your body. If necessary, repeat to keep the dog moving correctly. Never throw liver in the ring, for it will distract your dog and others when they are moving.

31

The process of throwing bait is a difficult one, and one that can produce good results only if done properly. Do not throw bait in the ring unless you have practiced at home. At home you may also train your dog to look forward by throwing small stones, for the dog will follow the noise. When in the ring, make the motion of throwing if you need something to get your dog started or to keep him moving. Remember this technique is not for every handler nor every dog, so be sure both you and your dog are trained and confident before you use this technique in the show ring.

When moving with your dog, the position and manner in which you hold the lead will be very important. While moving your dog, try to keep your left hand, with excess lead gathered in it, firmly closed. Hold your left arm slightly crooked and directly out from your body. This will keep the dog far enough away from your body so that he doesn't get under foot, but close enough to allow control and easy change of direction.

OFF THE HIP HEEL

This is a technique we have developed that allows you to keep the dog at a reasonable distance away from your body, approximately three feet, or the distance of your extended arm, never letting your dog move past your hip. This will teach the dog not to run past you and become uncontrollable. If your dog should try to pass you while moving, give him a correction by tugging on the lead and making a correction sound. Your dog will soon learn not to pass you when he is moving. This will also enable him to watch you and anticipate any turns you might be making. If your dog is moving in front of you, he cannot possibly see what you are about to do. This technique will make you appear as a more professional team.

TURNING YOUR DOG

Keeping your dog on a loose lead, and using the off-the-hip-heel technique, move approximately ten feet and make a turn to your right. At this time, you should signal your dog with a tug on the lead, a sound, and exaggerated body language. Body language is another useful form of communication between you and your dog. When training, dramatize, with your body, all the moves you are about to make. Keep repeating this technique until your dog understands what you are about to do. Then, when you are in the show ring, there will be no surprises or unexpected events your dog will have to contend with. Remember to praise and play with your dog after each of these training periods.

PATTERNS

It is a good idea to practice the patterns until you have mastered them. Do this by moving in the patterns without including your dog in the first practice sessions. After you are familiar with the patterns and shapes, and when to change hands and make turns, then practice with your dog.

When in the ring try to watch what the judge is requesting of the handlers and dogs ahead of you. Chances are good that you will be asked to move your dog the same way. If you are first in line, listen carefully to the judge's instructions. It is better to ask if you are uncertain what the judge wants you to do, rather than move incorrectly.

Always remember to keep your dog between yourself and the judge. Because judges sometimes request you to move your dog on a loose lead, make sure that your dog can move easily on a loose lead as well as a taut one. Remember to keep any surplus lead folded neatly in your hand. At home establish the speed of movement at which your dog looks best. When in the ring, try to move at the same speed.

"Around The Ring"

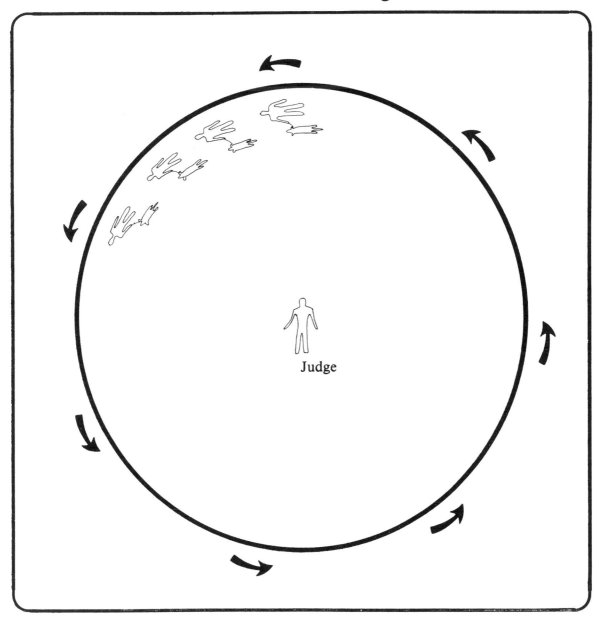

Judge

Often the judge will request the class of dogs to move around the ring together. The dogs will be moved around in a counterclockwise direction. You will always keep your dogs on the left side in this ring pattern. If you and your dog are at the head of the line and the judge requests the class to go around the ring together, it is a good idea to glance back at the rest of the dogs and handlers to make sure everyone is ready to begin. If you do not do this and someone in the line has been delayed or is slow starting up, you will have to halt and wait at this point anyway. If you are farther back in the line, allow ample space between yourself and the person in front of you. Do not crowd the person in front of you. If your dog is a fast mover, allow the handler and dog in front of you a few seconds "lead time." It is permissible and often necessary to request that the person and dog in back of you not follow too closely.

"Straight Down and Back"

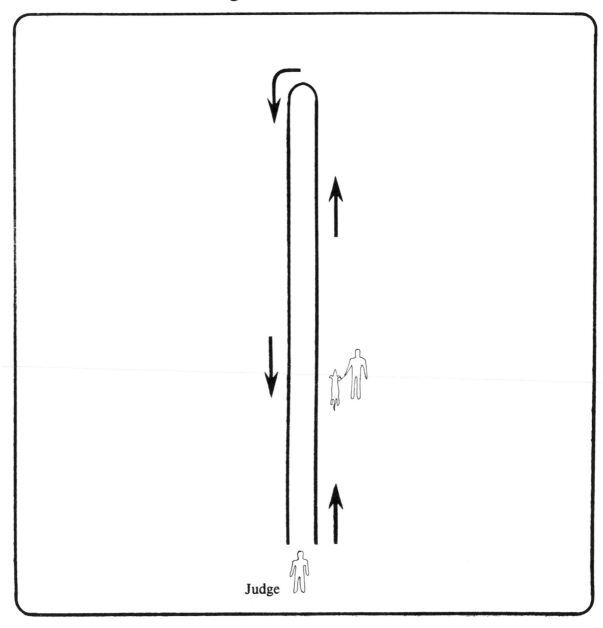

Judge

For individual gaiting a judge may sometimes ask you to move your dog "straight down and back." Make sure you establish eye contact with the judge so that you will move in a straight line away from the judge. When going away from the judge, pick a point in the ring and move toward it. When coming back toward the judge, be sure to glance toward him so that you don't run into him if he has changed position. Try to move your dog in as straight a line as possible. When com-

ing back, stop your dog in front of the judge and animate your dog by baiting him. You should always try to do this whenever you return to the judge after moving. In some cases, judges do not want dogs baited when they return from moving, but instead want you to return to the end of the line. If you have paid attention to the judge in earlier classes, you will be aware of his procedure.

"Triangle"

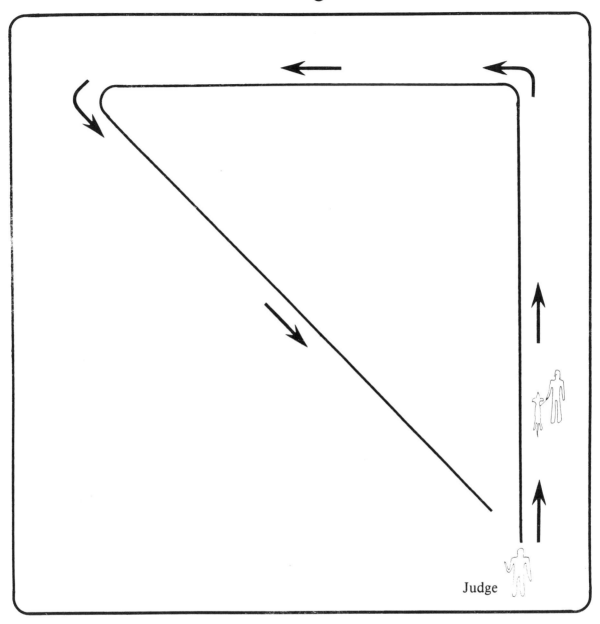

Judge

The triangle patterns are often selected for individual gaiting. In these patterns you will go to one end of the ring, make a 90° angle and turn, go to the other end of the ring and make a 45° angle and return to the judge. On the straight triangle pattern you will not have to change hands.

"Reverse Triangle"

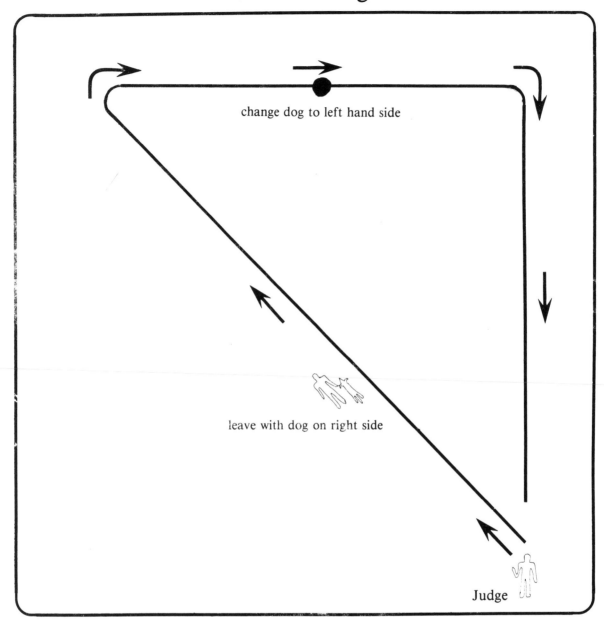

change dog to left hand side

leave with dog on right side

Judge

On the "reverse triangle," have the dog on your right side when you leave the judge so that you will need to change hands only once in the upper right corner of the triangle. At this point, change your dog to your left side and return to the judge. This change of hands must be made so as to enable you to bait your dog efficiently, for you will most likely train your dog and yourself to bait on the left side. Also, you will probably store the liver in your right-hand pocket.

"L"

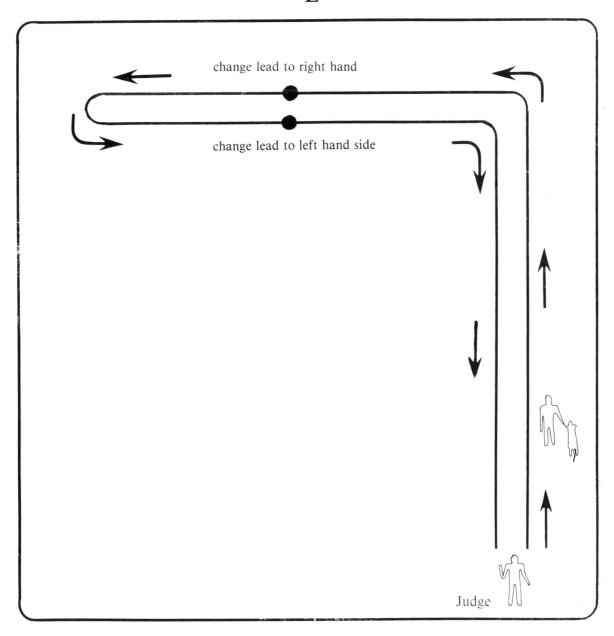

change lead to right hand

change lead to left hand side

Judge

For this pattern, an individual handler and dog will move straight away from the judge and make a 90° turn to the left. Before reaching the far end of the "L," put the lead in your right hand, letting your dog stay on your left; now turn so the dog and lead are on your right-hand side, giving the judge a continued view of your dog. You must remember never to block the judge's view of your dog. When returning from the opposite end of the top of the "L," return the dog to your left hand side and return to the judge.

"Reverse L"

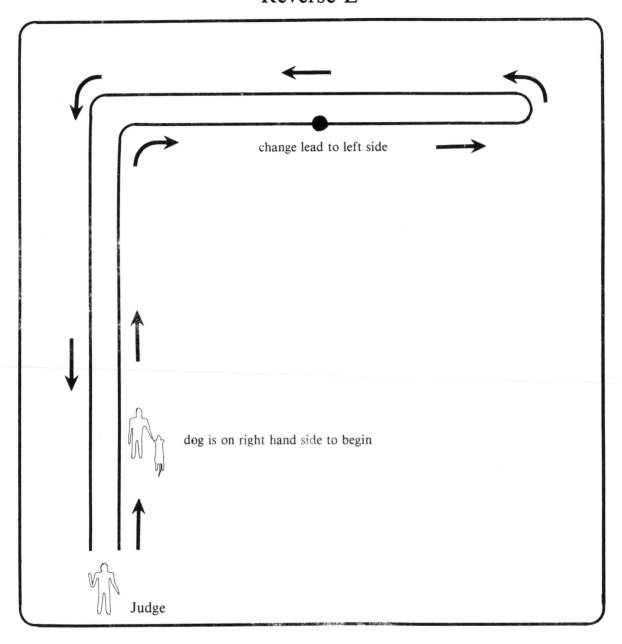

change lead to left side

dog is on right hand side to begin

Judge

This pattern is often used in Junior Showmanship but is rarely used in the breed ring. Go away from the judge with your dog on the right-hand side, make a 90° turn to your right and before reaching the end of the "L," put the lead in your left hand and start making the turn. When you have made your turn, the dog should be on your left side and you will be ready to go back across the top of the "L" and then return to the judge.

"T"

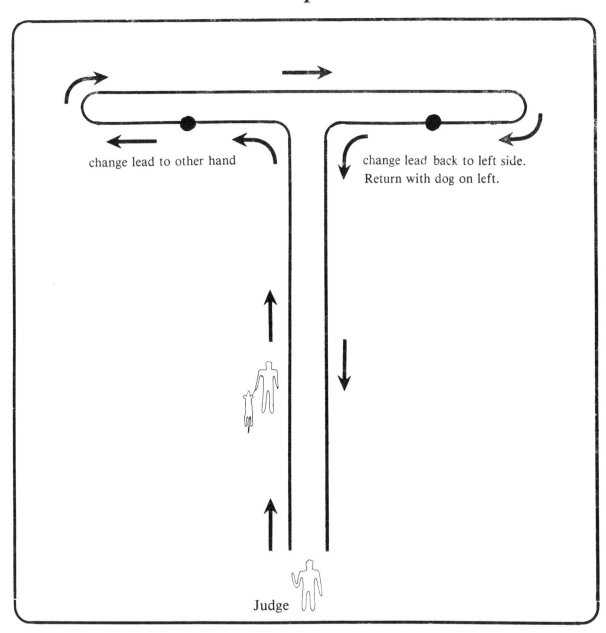

change lead to other hand

change lead back to left side.
Return with dog on left.

Judge

This pattern of individual gait requires the dog and handler to move straight away to a point at the far side of the ring. The dog will be on the left-hand side. At the top of the "T," make a 90° turn to the left, go across the top of the "T" and as you approach the end, put the lead in your right hand, with the dog remaining on your left. Turn around facing the opposite direction. The dog is now on your right. Note that the dog has changed direction, not changed position, but you have turned around. With the dog on your right-hand side, start across the top of the "T," passing the center of the "T" and continuing across to the other end. Now transfer the lead to the left hand, and turn and go in the opposite direction. The dog is now on the left. The dog has not changed position but only direction and you have turned around. Go to the center of the "T" with the dog on your left-hand side and then return to the judge.

Always return to the judge with the dog on your left side so that you can effectively bait him when you stop in front of the judge. Pull the bait out of your pocket prior to stopping in front of the judge.

40

Glance back at the judge, making eye contact, before moving your dog.

Make certain the lead is in the correct position and give the dog a signal (either hand or verbal) that you are ready to begin moving.

When returning to the judge make sure to establish eye-contact.

Stop your dog in front of the judge and bait your dog until the judge is through looking at him.

Keep your dog moving in a straight line back to the judge.

Move the dog away from the judge. Pick a point at the far end of the ring and move toward it.

Glance up before reaching the judge to make sure he has not changed position and that he does not have further instructions.

When baiting your dog while you are standing, you should be an approximate distance of three feet, or the length of your extended leg, away from the dog.

The loose lead approach to baiting is accomplished by holding the liver away from the dog near your waist. The collar should be loose and the lead should be slack.

5
Baiting Your Dog

Baiting serves the purpose of gaining your dog's attention and holding it for a period of time. Baiting can aid in helping your dog to maintain a stacked position or to strike a desirable pose when standing in front of the judge, or after stopping in front of the judge after moving in the ring. Baiting your dog without prior stacking is referred to as "free baiting."

Bait can refer to any small edible food for use in the ring with the purpose of gaining your dog's attention. Liver is the most effective and commonly used form of bait because it is not costly and is clean to handle, and it can be easily preserved. Squeaky toys are sometimes used to gain a dog's attention but are not desirable in the show ring because they distract and may irritate other dogs. Also, squeaky toys cannot be used as a form of reward whereas a piece of liver can be given to the dog and will be most appreciated.

Baiting should be taught to a dog after he has been lead broken and has learned to hold a stacked position. However, teaching a young puppy not to jump up on you when you give him a treat around the house is a good way to start teaching him informally some of the basics of baiting. At no time, during puppy or adult training, allow your dog to pick up any treats or bait from the ground.

A good method for preparing liver is:

• Select beef or pork liver

• Wash liver thoroughly

• Place in boiling water and let boil rapidly thirty minutes. Add garlic or onion flavoring if your dog likes the taste.

• Remove liver from boiling water, wash off, and pat dry.

• Place liver in a pan and place in 375° oven for twenty minutes baking on EACH side.

• Remove and refrigerate or pack in salt as an extended preservative for long trips.

From either a stacked position or a natural stance, the dog should maintain a reasonable distance, approximately three feet, from the handler. A distance equal to the approximate length of your extended leg enables the dog to have easy sight and smell of the bait. This distance will also encourage the dog to lean forward and will allow the judge to get a clear view of the dog.

Teach your dog to play catch with the bait. Do not let him pick up from the ground any bait that he does not catch.

Playing catch in the ring will add to your dog's enjoyment and fun in the ring. Also, this is an excellent way to animate your dog and help him to relax.

There are two general methods used in baiting. The loose lead approach is accomplished by holding the liver away from the dog about as high as your waist and having the lead slack and the collar loose. As a rule, this is more effective for a well-trained show dog because such a dog will maintain his position easily. When using the loose lead approach, start teaching your dog to catch bait, keeping in mind never to let him pick up anything he doesn't catch. This will become a game and add to the fun and excitement your dog will exhibit in the show ring. The other method is the tight lead approach. It is accomplished by holding the lead set in a tight position high on the neck in order to steady the dog and maintain the stacked position. In this approach, the liver is held almost directly in front of the dog's head so as to gain his attention. This method also enables the handler to position the dog so as to accent the dog's strong points and hide any faults.

The intent in using bait is to hold the dog's attention.

However, only small bits need to be dispensed to the dog. Liver can be kept in a small plastic bag in a pocket of your clothing, tucked in your arm band, or held in the mouth, so that both hands can be free while you are in the ring working with the dog. Remember, you are baiting your dog and not others, and you will find you may upset both the judge and other exhibitors by throwing or leaving excess liver around the show ring.

The position in which you hold the liver will vary with the size of the breed. However, always remember to hold the liver so that the dog's head is kept in as straight and as flattering a position as possible.

Teaching your dog not to dive to the ground for any dropped bait is very important. We have tried to stress this point because if yours is the last class to enter the ring, the ground may be littered with liver and cause you many problems. Also, the judge will not get a complete view of your dog if he is diving toward the ground for bait.

The other method of baiting is called the tight lead approach. Hold the collar high on the neck to help maintain the stacked position. Hold the liver almost directly in front of the dog's head so as to gain and hold his attention.

BEST OF
BREED

COMBINED SPECIALTY
CLUBS OF ATLANTA
APRIL 1981
PHOTOS BY ALVERSON

6

Hiding Faults

After reading the Standard and the history of your breed, you undoubtedly will find that the dog you are showing does not fit the Standard in every way. So let us accept the fact that your dog is not perfect. You must also understand that the dogs you are competing against also are not perfect. It is the judge's task to discover your dog's good points and weak points. The judge is only human, and in the approximately two and a half minutes allocated to him to evaluate your dog, you cannot expect him to find all of your dog's good points. Unfortunately, it is usually apparent immediately what lesser qualities your dog may possess. Therefore, this chapter is devoted to helping you to minimize your dog's obvious weak points, often referred to as faults.

FAULTS APPARENT WHILE A DOG IS STANDING (IN STACKED POSITION)

Fault	*How to Correct It or Minimize It*
Leaning back (or shying) during judge's examination	Place right hand under collar at top of neck, and place left hand firmly behind head at top of neck.
Leaning back while judge is standing at a distance	Place right hand on collar with collar at top of neck, and place left hand on tail pushing forward.
Swayback or sagging topline	Place front feet further under shoulders than normal. Left hand should push stomach upward while setting left rear leg.
Front feet turning out	Refer to chapter on stacking your dog, and while setting the left leg, turn it inward. Do the same with the right front let.
Cow hocked (rear legs leaning inward toward one another)	Refer to chapter on stacking your dog. Hold the collar at the top of the neck with right hand, have left hand nearly underneath the stomach of the dog and grasp the left rear leg, bending the hock outward (away from the other leg). Then grasp the right rear leg and repeat the same process. This procedure may have to be repeated in your daily training program in order to achieve a degree of success.
Down in pastern	Generally this is a hereditary problem but this condition can be caused by a calcium deficiency or lack of exercise, or both. To correct this condition we suggest you first consult your veterinarian and try feeding your dog with the food pan elevated to the point where your dog must stretch upward in order to reach the food. To hide this fault while stacking your dog, place the front feet further under the shoulders than they normally would be placed. Then lift some of the weight off the pasterns either by placing the collar at the top of the neck and lifting upward, or in the case of breeds shown without a collar, lift the head upward and hold the weight off the pasterns with your hand.
High in the rear (rear higher than shoulders/withers)	When setting up the rear legs, spread the legs apart and extend them 1 to 3 inches further back, depending on the degree of the fault.

FAULTS WHILE DOG IS MOVING

Sidewinding	This fault occurs when your dog does not move in a straight line, but moves either with the front end too close to you or with the rear end too close to you, making the dog appear to be moving sideways. This is corrected by training. Move your dog first on the left side and then on the right side. This can also be helped by the off-the-hip heel technique we discussed in the section on movement.

Pacing

This is when, while gaiting, the left front and left rear legs of the dog move in unison, and the right front and right rear legs move in unison. To correct this fault, signal your dog while gaiting by giving him a sharp "tug" on the lead, pulling him off balance. Continuing this method in your training program should enable you to minimize the problem.

In general, all of the other moving faults displayed by dogs can usually be attributed directly to the fact that most people use their lead as a "tow chain" and keep the collar position too high and too tight around the neck. Repeatedly pulling the dog off stride (out of proper gait), and at times actually lifting the front feet off the ground, often prevents the judge from being able to evaluate movement properly.

To correct such faults, use the off-the-hip heel technique, letting the lead hang loosely while gaiting your dog in the ring. The only time the lead should tighten is when you are signaling your dog to speed up, slow down, or turn.

FAULTS WHILE DOG IS BAITING

Baiting too closely

Loose lead baiting should always be performed with a distance of three feet or more between the dog and the handler. A distance closer than three feet will cause the dog to pull his head back in order to see the liver, making the topline to appear weak, and giving the judge a generally poor picture of your dog.

Diving for liver

There is nothing more disturbing in the ring than to have your dog "dive" to the ground and try to pick up a piece of bait. Correcting this fault can be accomplished by training your dog to never pick up anything from the floor or ground. You should also consider your fellow exhibitor and not leave bait on the ground when you are in the ring.

Breaking gait because of inappropriate baiting

Handlers frequently endeavor to bait their dogs while moving. This generally causes the dog to sidewind and try to jump up and grab the bait while moving. To eliminate this problem, train your dog at home to catch a ball. After he has learned to catch the ball, start throwing the ball (and later the bait) out away from him. Do not enable him to retrieve it. When in the ring, use the same method of throwing, but use bait, not the ball. You will find that the dog now will move in a more animated fashion *and* in a straight line.

Move your dog in the patterns the judge requests. Stop in front of the judge after moving your dog so that the judge can examine him further. Move to the end of the line only after you are directed to do so.

Skillful handling and ring strategy produce these results.

7

Ring Strategy

In the world of show dogs everyone likes to be a winner, and most strive very hard to achieve their show goals. One of the best ways to achieve your show goals is through good ring strategy. Many amateur and professional handlers have no strategy at all. This situation should be avoided. The following is a discussion of several strategy tips to use when preparing for the ring.

WATCHING RING PROCEDURE

As a rule, there is an expected sequence for judging in any show ring. To be sure what procedure the judge for your breed is following, go to his ring early and watch him judge other breeds if at all possible. Also, try to watch his ring procedure when *your* breed is in the ring. One caution to note is that most judges will examine your dog's mouth. As a rule, you should show the dog's bite and teeth to the judge. Don't wait for him to reach for the mouth and open it. A judge must review many mouths a day, and the potential for transmitting disease, infection, or illness from one dog to another is apparent. Also, you never know if a judge may have shaving lotion or cleansing alcohol upon his hands or wrists, possibly causing the dog to sneeze or give an abnormal reaction to the scent. By showing the mouth yourself, you have more control of the situation and it is less likely that your dog will shy from the judge. It will also minimize the chance, no matter how remote you feel the chance may be, that your dog will bite the judge.

ENTERING THE RING

Upon entering the ring, the steward may require you to be in catalog order, which means by lowest armband number to highest in your class. You will be directed to a certain line or area within the ring in which to set up or stack your dog. If you first look for a suitable, flat piece of ground, your dog will appear better stacked and more comfortable during judging. To accomplish this, survey the ring during several classes before you are to enter the ring, so that you can locate the good spots and avoid slopes, gulleys, and high ground.

If you are able to choose the place in line where you will be stacking and moving your dog, there are several points to consider. It is possible (but does not always happen) that a judge will leave the first dog in line as first place, but you must be very alert if you choose this position. If you have a dog who spooks easily or is uneasy about sounds of other dogs behind him, try to be last in line in order to provide your dog with a less-threatening environment.

While in the ring, the most important thing you want to accomplish is to make sure the judge views your dog as well as possible so whether stacked, free baited, or moving, your dog should appear at his best. When you are moving up in line during examination or for individual gait, always set your dog up in the spot where the previous person's dog was judged. Whenever the judge is able to view your dog, he is evaluating him, so if you are not stacking or baiting your dog, you may be giving the judge

Remember to always try to show your dog's mouth to the judge yourself. This reduces the chance of your dog shying from the judge.

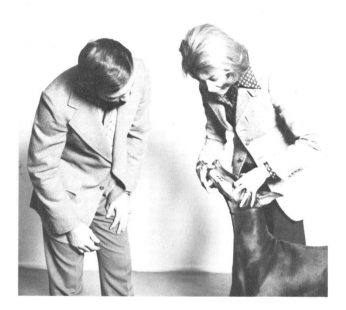

a bad view. Before entering the ring, do not stand in a position where the judge can easily see your dog.

Always keep your dog under control. In the case of a male, be very careful not to allow him to get too close to another male or a bitch in season. If there is a bitch in season in the ring, a bit of Vapo Rub placed in each nostril of the male will minimize the chances of his becoming upset or unruly.

When out of sight of the judge, do not forget to play with your dog. Let him jump up on you to relax and calm him.

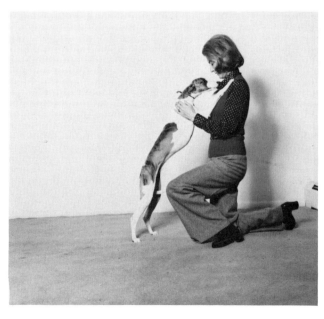

CONFIDENCE: THE ATTITUDE YOU PROJECT

A winner usually tries to show enthusiasm and confidence. The serious, dedicated show person should exhibit a winning attitude whether he wins or loses on any one day. He should start with an attitude of objectivity and courtesy toward exhibitors and judges and end with a positive "I'm glad I won" or "Well, I did the best I could" attitude. As an exhibitor, you have everything to gain by showing a positive attitude in the ring to all concerned.

While in the ring, remain calm and unhurried, no matter what happens. If you can remain composed, your dog will relax and your chances of winning will improve. Even if you have close "down to the wire" competition that day, it is important always to keep trying, for many decisions against a dog are due to a handler not giving that extra effort. That little extra effort may just be the *winning* edge.

Some of the classes you will be exhibiting in will be very large. The tension of being alert for a long period will wear on many dogs. Playing with your dog will help relieve this tension for both you and him.

SIZING UP AND OVERCOMING THE COMPETITION

After you have entered the ring and your dog has been initially reviewed by the judge, begin sizing up your opposition. Don't take too much time doing this; just a glance will suffice for starters. Make sure you know the good points of the dog you are showing. Make yourself well aware of the breed history and Standard so that you know the good points and the faults on which the judge must base the awards.

JUDGING PREFERENCES

Based on a judge's preferences, you can begin accentuating a dog's strong points. Expertise in making eye contact and in projecting your dog's good points become particularly important when the judge has narrowed his choice down to two or three dogs, and is comparing specific points from one to another. By looking at a particular good point on your dog, or aiming your body to that particular part of the dog, you will subtly draw the judge's attention to that area.

Every judge knows the Standard of the breed he is judging, but how he ranks specific points of the Standard against the competition on a particular day may vary. Be alert as to the judge's preferences and comparisons with competition in the breed.

As the judge begins approaching your dog for examination, make sure your dog is well presented. Note that the second and third dogs are already set to be examined. Always be aware of the position of the judge.

Although the judge has left the first dog, the person handling the dog should keep his dog stacked in case the judge turns around for another look.

The judge is now examining the third dog and the first two handlers in line are still working with their dogs. That little extra effort may be the *winning edge.*

Project the good points of your dog, give them special emphasis by looking directly at them.

It is apparent what the handler of this dog is projecting by aiming his body and looking toward the front section of the dog.

Angle your body toward the area of the dog you want the judge to notice.

POSITION OF THE JUDGE

At all times know where the judge is standing in the ring so that you can have your dog stacked or free baited into a natural stance to its best advantage. Don't stare at the judge, but try to make eye contact at various intervals if possible, for this shows alertness and interest. If a judge walks down the line of stacked dogs, be aware that he may ask you to move to another position or gait your dog again. If the judge has moved other dogs for further consideration, when he approaches your dog, it is wise to appear as if you expect to be moved next.

If a judge positions two dogs together and asks them to be moved together, try to be first out so that you can leave the judge with your dog on the right. The judge will want the dogs to move side by side. This means that when the dogs come back to the judge, your dog will be on the left, and you will be in a better position to bait your dog in front of the judge than will your competitor.

It is important to know where the judge is standing so that you can relax your dog by playing with him, letting him jump up on you, or whatever reduces the tension for him. Another reason to know the judge's location is that if there is a big class, you will also want the dog out of the judge's sight and you can "hide" by moving back behind the others in line when you are not near the judge. Do not spend time in the ring talking to fellow exhibitors or persons outside the ring because this shows a lack of concern and interest as to what is happening in the ring. Always remember that the judge is the one to whom you should be directing your attention, for this will pay off the most.

Go to your place and set up your dog. Have your dog at his best while in direct view of the judge.

Move up in line and set your dog up again in front of the judge. Notice that the handler has his dog set and ready for examination before the handler and dog in front of him start moving away.

Always have your dog well presented during examination. Baiting will encourage your dog to show animation while retaining his show stance or pose.

Steady your dog during the judge's examination to ensure that everything goes smoothly.

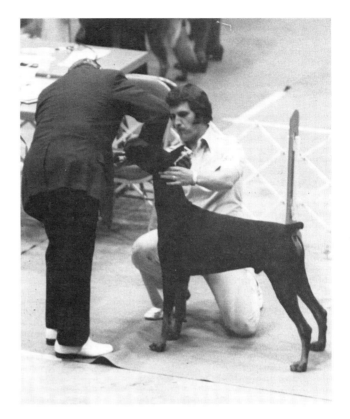

CONCLUSION

Ring strategy is one of the ingredients necessary to produce a winning attitude in and out of the ring. Your mind must be focused upon the task at hand, and your motions should be of a controlled, precise nature. Be consistent in your approaches and strategy and do not change them from show to show or week to week. Your dog will appreciate the consistency and so will the judge.

Try never to be above constructive creative criticism or helpful hints about showing your dog. We have never met a successful person showing dogs, whether amateur or professional, that was not ready and anxious to learn.

Go back in line and set your dog up again. Be prepared to move your dog again or change placement in the line.

A crate is a necessary item for your show dog. Most dogs enjoy their crate and will go into it readily.

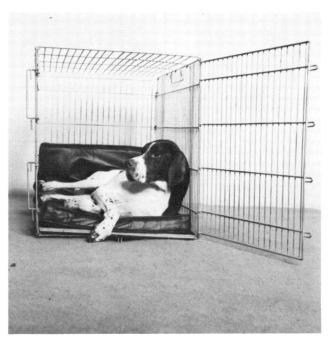

The crate should be large enough so the dog can lie down comfortably.

It is important that the crate be neither too large nor too small.

An exercise pen can be set up for your dog while travelling or at the shows. Be sure your dog is aware of the purpose of the exercise pen by also setting it up occasionally at home.

8

Necessary Show Equipment

As any good craftsman will agree, the tools of the trade are of the utmost importance if one is to perform good work. Without proper tools, correctly used, it is difficult to produce the best possible results. The same is true with the "tools" or equipment you will need to aid you in showing your dog. The kind of equipment necessary can be divided into two categories—equipment to be used in the ring and equipment to be used outside the ring. However, since both will affect your dog's show performance, both types are of equal importance.

CRATES

A crate is one of the most necessary items for your show dog. In selecting the correct crate for your dog, size should be the first consideration. Since well-made crates can be costly, if you own a puppy, purchase a crate that will be the correct size when he has matured fully to adult size. An adult dog should be able to stand up, turn around easily, and lie down comfortably in his crate. It is important that the crate be neither too small nor too large.

There are numerous types of crates available—wire, plastic, wooden, metal, and combinations thereof. Be sure that the crate you buy is steady, is from a well-known manufacturer of crates, and is escape-proof. Dogs have been known to hurt themselves trying to escape from crates. If you ship your dog by air, you should know that most dogs, except for the smallest breeds, must travel in the aircraft baggage compartment in airline-approved crates. Keep this in mind when selecting a crate so that you don't end up purchasing two crates instead of one.

Crates are valuable in a variety of situations—car travel, training, housebreaking, and temporary confinement. Your dog will appreciate a place of his own and the crate will serve this purpose. Then, when you are at the dog shows, your dog will consider his crate a "home away from home," and will stay quiet and calm so that he will be rested when he walks into the ring. Never at any time punish your dog by putting him in his crate.

FEED AND WATER CONTAINERS

The choice of appropriate feed and water dishes is also important. The correct size and shape for your breed must be kept in mind. For example, Boxers, Bulldogs, and breeds with faces of similar type need dishes with wide bottoms, while Spaniels, Poodles, and other long-eared breeds can use a more tapered bowl to keep their ears from hanging in the food. The food and water pans should be made from non-toxic materials that will not break or crack under normal use. They should be easy to clean and dry (and disinfect if necessary). For this reason stainless steel or heavy duty plastic dishes are suggested. A variety of hook-on crate pans and water bottles are available and useful because they cannot tip over.

EXERCISE PENS

Another necessary piece of dog show equipment is the exercise pen. Portable, heavy gauge wire pens, can be ordered in a variety of sizes and heights, and, if needed, floors and covers. For travelling, and at the shows where space is often limited, setting up an exercise pen is an excellent way to allow your dog some place to stretch his legs and go to the bathroom.

Another necessary piece of show equipment is a tack box, which can hold grooming equipment, leads and collars, and other show related items.

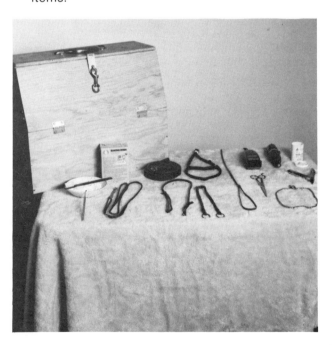

LEADS AND COLLARS

There are many excellent show leads and collars available. The proper lead for your dog will depend upon his breed type and age, and how well-trained and controllable your dog is. As a general rule, the lighter and simpler the collar and lead arrangement, the easier to deal with in the ring. One-piece leads and collars are good for the breeds where the lead is removed for stacking.

Remember, show leads are for the show ring and are generally not safe for use as an everyday walking lead. Be sure to buy a heavy duty walking lead for daily use.

GROOMING EQUIPMENT

In Chapter 9 we discussed the types of grooming equipment available. It is a good idea to buy whatever you will need to groom your dog properly, and then to prepare a duplicate kit of supplies to take with you whenever travelling to the shows. Refer to a pre-show checklist prior to leaving for the show to make sure you have everything you will need.

SPECIAL WEATHER NEEDS

Depending upon the weather, various show equipment needs will change. For the warmer days, you will need an ice chest, water pan (both filled with ice), and an atomizer spray bottle filled with water. These should be used to keep the dog cool by spraying water in the mouth, or by feeding ice cubes.

For the short coated breeds, a towel soaked in a solution of four parts water to one part vinegar and placed on the dog's coat is another means of cooling. For all breeds, the best idea on a hot day is to find shade for your dog and keep him there as much as possible. This may mean that you will place the dog in a small patch of shade that you will make with your own shadow.

Colder weather can be coped with by providing a coat or blanket to wrap your dog in when he is not in the ring. Of course, you will always avoid having your dog stand around in the cold unnecessarily prior to entering the ring.

On a cold day or a rainy day, provide a coat or sweater for your dog. If you have a small dog, hold him under your own coat where he can be further protected from the weather.

For hot days, a wet towel is ideal for the short coated breeds. Keeping your dog quiet during warm weather is a good idea. This will result in a calmer and more rested dog when it is his turn to go into the ring.

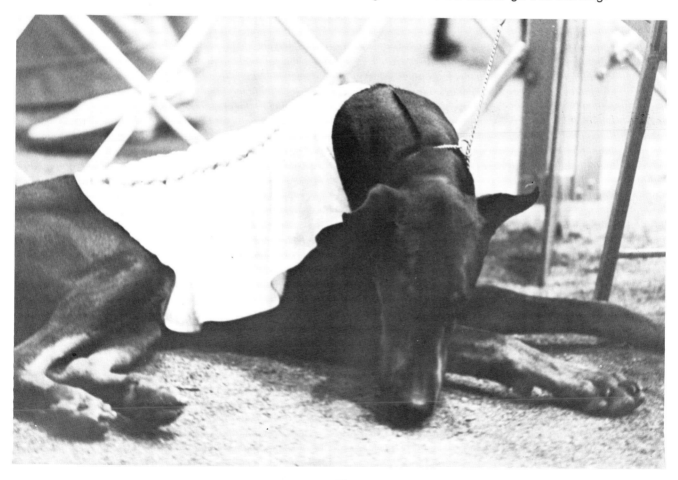

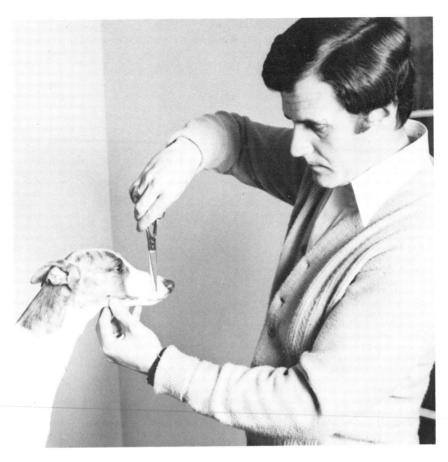

Whiskers can be removed with the scissors.

9
Grooming Your Show Dog

The grooming of a dog's coat for the show ring is becoming more elaborate every year. New grooming products and their claims of desirable results are constantly appearing on the market, sometimes resulting in confusion for the show dog owner. The breeds and their grooming needs are so different that it would take hundreds of pages to point out specifically how to groom each one for the show ring. Many individual breed books are available for this purpose. This chapter simply will identify the basics of good grooming and further acquaint the show dog owner with some of the available products and equipment.

Cleanliness of the dog is the foundation for grooming activities for every breed. Nothing is more disturbing to the judge than to be presented with a dirty dog. The term dirty refers to the condition and state of cleanliness of the dog's coat, skin, eyes, ears, teeth, and feet. If you are following the health care procedure discussed in Chapter 13, you are already taking many of the steps necessary for good grooming. The following paragraphs offer additional suggestions to expand and refine your grooming techniques, procedures, and knowledge.

SHAMPOOS AND GROOMING AIDS

Shampoos and grooming aids consist of the following type products:

- All purpose/specialized foam shampoos: pH balanced for dogs, formulated to clean the hair thoroughly and rinse out easily.

- Cream rinses: formulated to condition and make the hair more manageable after the bath.

- Tangle removers: designed to help remove tangles by reducing brushing and combing time, and to help minimize the dog's discomfort while mats and snarls are being removed.

- Coat conditioners: brushing and conditioning aids to keep the hair lustrous and in optimum condition and to help to restore damaged hair to a healthy state.

- Coat dressings: anti-static aids for long coats; non-oily and non-sticky, these dressings leave the coat more manageable and less likely to be fly-away.

- Grooming powders/whiteners/dry cleaners: to clean the hair, to help remove surface stains, and to cut excessive oils and dirt.

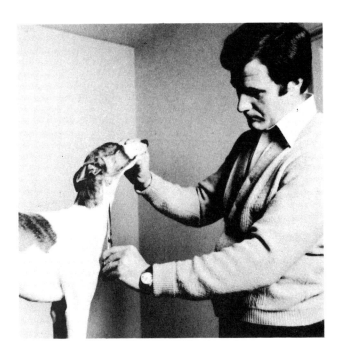

Keep a firm grip on your dog while he is being scissored or at any time he is on the grooming table.

In selecting grooming products, especially shampoos, the correct pH value is of vital importance in keeping a dog's coat in optimum condition. The pH value of a liquid is an indication of its acidity or alkalinity. The degree of acidity or alkalinity is measured on a scale having a range of pH values from 0 to 14, with a pH value of 7 being neutral, or neither acid nor alkaline.

The pH for the human skin and hair is in the 4.5 to 5.5 range, or on the acid side. The dog's skin and hair are not the same as those of a human. The pH for the dog's skin and hair is considerably different and more alkaline, falling in the range of 6.2 to 8.6. Variations can occur depending on the breed, age, and physical condition. This may seem rather technical but it simply means that the dog's hair and skin are at their healthiest in this range, for that is when the coat has its greatest elasticity, strength, and luster.

To maintain the skin and coat at their very best, grooming products, especially shampoos, should be properly pH balanced for dogs, not only for better cleaning, a higher gloss, and healthier coat, but also to protect the skin. Unfortunately, many people think that human shampoos are best for dogs. This is a misconception, and overuse of such products can cause problems, especially for the show coat, for they do not effectively clean and condition the hair.

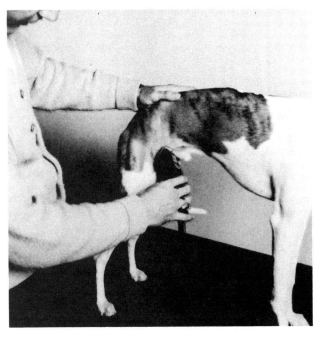

A motor driven clipper is being used here for trimming excess hair around the loin. Be certain to familiarize yourself with the instructions for use of the clipper.

68

Nails can be shortened speedily by using a guillotine clipper. Because you may cut nails too closely occasionally, and reach the quick of the nail, be sure to have a blood arresting agent in case you need to clot the nail to prevent bleeding.

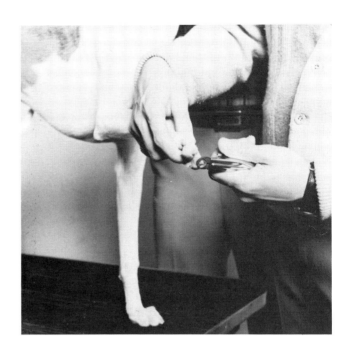

GROOMING EQUIPMENT

A variety of equipment is available for grooming use—tables, dryers, clippers and clipper accessories, nail trimmers, combs, brushes, scissors, and other aids for grooming individual breeds. Choice of proper grooming equipment is important. Regardless of the dog's breed, it is necessary to have the correct grooming equipment and to know how to use it properly. If you were to ask professionals about the purchase of grooming tools, the majority would advise investing in the best quality grooming equipment you could afford. The correct and best quality equipment saves time and produces better results.

A sturdy grooming table should be one of your first investments. From puppyhood, a dog of any breed, long or smooth-coated, should be trained to stand or lie quietly on the table while it is being groomed. A good quality table should be steady and firm and the top should be covered with non-slip material.

Also available are professional stand and cage dryers. The type you select should depend on how many dogs you groom regularly, what type coats they have, how often they are shampooed, and the sizes of the dogs. If you own a single dog, an ordinary blow dryer will be sufficient if you need to dry the coat.

Several different types of motor driven clippers are available. Whatever type of clipper you choose, read the instructions for correct operation and maintenance procedures to ensure its smooth performance. There are fine quality scissors for all types of grooming—barber scissors with long straight blades tapering to a point and grooming shears with detachable blades are available. For scissoring fussy animals or for trimming around the eyes, ears, muzzle, or other sensitive areas, we suggest using blunt-tip curved scissors, for they are ideal for this type of trimming.

An electric nail grinder is used by many people in preparing a dog for the show ring. Grind both sides of each nail until you reach the desired length of nail. Grind from the top and bottom of the nail to form an arrowhead shape. Through normal wear the nail will round itself.

Proper attire is important if you are going to be exhibiting your dog in the ring. for men, a sports jacket, or suit, with a shirt and tie, is always in good taste.

For women, pants with a blazer and shirt, or pantsuit, is ideal. Clothing should be selected so that it has a right hand pocket to hold bait or other in-the-ring equipment.

Combs are available in various styles with or without handles, for all types of grooming. The type and tooth spacing of the comb you select should depend on your breed and its coat texture, but generally, fine combs are used for sparse or silky hair and medium tooth combs are for coats of average texture.

The type and texture of the dog's coat are also important in the selection of brushes. For your selection, many types of brushes are available to choose from, including:

• Pin brushes: available in various sizes and recommended for long-coated breeds; each style has polished pins with rounded ends to prevent scratching the skin.

• Bristle brushes: with natural or a combination of natural and nylon bristles are available.

To cut nails efficiently there are three different types of equipment: 1. an electric nail grinder; 2. a guillotine nail trimmer; and 3. a file. The method we have found most effective is using the nail grinder.

It is necessary to know the ideal appearance of your breed(s). You must also know which tools are necessary and how to use the equipment correctly. It is suggested that you read or purchase one of the many books written by experts in the field, describing the histories, grooming, and show presentation of the various breeds.

There exists a set of unwritten rules concerning dog shows. At the core of most of the "rules of etiquette" is courtesy. Courtesy must be extended to the judge, to fellow exhibitors, and also to the dogs that are being shown. Dressing well and behaving with good taste are among other unwritten rules for a dog show.

PROPER ATTIRE

To provide yourself with any advantage you can gain in the show ring, begin with appropriate dress. Your choice of clothing can affect your performance in the ring greatly, and thus will affect your dog's chances of winning. Clothing can be selected to enhance your dog's appearance. If you are showing more than one dog, wear neutral colors appropriate for all your dogs. A darker-colored outfit for a white or light-colored dog, or a light set of clothing for dark-colored dogs can make a nice appearance. Try not to choose clothes for dog shows that will clash with your dog. For example, an unwise selection of clothing might be the choice of a black and white polka dot dress to exhibit a Dalmatian. In general, try not to select clothes that are too dark because they will show dust very easily. The same is also true of clothes that are too light in color.

A courtesy you should always extend to fellow exhibitors at the show is keeping your dog under control. Do not block ring entrances and exits. Keep your dog on a short lead, close to your side.

After the judge has awarded you a placement make some signal or gesture to acknowledge that you understand.

Always be polite and courteous to the judge, and do not forget to thank him for your ribbon.

Avoid tight clothing, for it will impair your movement in the ring. Stay away from loose fitting garments which may flap around while you are in the ring and disturb your dog.

For men, the choice of a suit or sports jacket, and shirt and tie is always appropriate. Women should choose simple dresses, a skirt and blouse combination, or pantsuit. Slacks with a blazer and blouse are the ideal combination. A right-hand pocket is necessary to hold in-the-ring equipment, so clothing should be selected with this in mind. Sensible shoes with crepe or rubber soles are necessary. Never wear high heeled shoes or shoes with platform soles in the ring.

Avoid wearing excessive jewelry. It will make unnecessary noise and it may get tangled in the lead or otherwise interfere with effectively showing your dog.

ARMBANDS

Pick up your armband at least ten minutes before your class is called. Once you have received your armband, check the number and class you are entered in against the steward's catalog to make sure you have the correct one. Turn your armband over to the reverse side and write your show information on it, such as breed, class, and your dog's name. Then put a small tear in the middle of the right and left side. Put two comfortable fitting rubber bands on your arm and put the armband under the rubber bands. Be sure that the armband fits in the tears on either side of the armband. If you follow this procedure, it will keep you from losing your arm-band in the ring.

Report any absences you may have to the ring steward. Make sure that your armband is well-secured and in full view on the upper left side of your arm when you enter the ring. If you are able to see your armband, so is the judge. After the placements have been made at the conclusion of judging and you have received a placement, go over to the designated place in the ring and have your arm band in full view when the judge's book is to be marked.

RING COURTESY

When you enter the ring, do so in a courteous and orderly manner. In an increasing number of dog shows, judges are requiring that you enter the ring in numerical order. If the judge does not require that you enter the ring in numerical order, we suggest that you use common sense in choosing your ring position. If you have a large, fast-moving dog, try to go to the front of the line. If you have a small, slow-moving puppy, go to the back of the line, where you will not hold back the rest of the dogs moving around the ring.

Set your dog up at a reasonable distance in back or in front of another dog. Remember not to gait too closely when moving around the ring. In general, do not engage in any actions which will distract another dog or another handler.

COURTESY TO JUDGE

Always show the utmost patience, courtesy, and attention in your attitude when in the ring. If the judge gives you directions that you do not understand, politely ask the judge to repeat them.

When awarded a placement, make an acknowledgement, such as a nod of the head or gesture with hand to let the judge know that you are aware of his decision. When handed a ribbon, thank the judge and move out of the ring unless remaining for further competition. Keep a close eye on the judge when stacking or gaiting your dog, for he may give further instructions.

As a closing note, here are several show ring courtesies and rules to be aware of:

• Do not wear a hat or any inappropriate attire in the ring.

• Do not attempt to conceal a fault of your dog. Likewise, do not over-emphasize a good point that your dog may have, for the judge may find such action insulting. (This is referred to by many as "painting pictures in the ring.")

• Do not stare at the judge. Pay close attention to him.

• Do not converse at all with the judge except in response to questions or to ask that instructions be repeated.

• Do not discuss your dog's show wins or pedigree with the judge, unless he asks.

• Do not argue with the judge or question him about his decision.*

• Do not require that the judge handle the dog's mouth. If possible offer and show the dog's mouth yourself.

With all these suggestions and facts firmly in mind, you should be ready to exhibit your dog with proper etiquette and poise.

---

*These actions could result in disciplinary proceedings being brought against you by the judge, the show-giving club, or The American Kennel Club. Above all, they are in poor taste and are not consistent with a sportsmanlike attitude.

11
Junior Showmanship

Junior Showmanship competition is an excellent means of training young ladies and gentlemen in the art of handling and the sport of showing dogs. The proper attitude is very important in the world of dog shows, and Junior Showmanship emphasizes and encourages courteous, sportsmanlike behavior.

There are very few adults who can appreciate the hard work and enthusiasm that go into being a successful Junior handler. Because this area of competition is judged by the ability and skill with which a dog is presented, rather than the quality of the dog, it maximizes the importance of proper presentation because, in Junior Showmanship, the competitors are always working toward developing their skills. A wrong move, a lapse of attention, or a signal not noticed can be the difference between being first or being unplaced in the class.

It is important for the Junior to be knowledgeable about the breed Standard of the dog he is showing, general dog show terms, and elementary dog anatomy for judges frequently ask questions on these topics. It is too bad that the criteria for judging Junior Showmanship differ so vastly from those of the conformation ring. The "T" pattern, regularly used in the Junior Showmanship ring, is rarely used in the conformation ring. It would be more beneficial to the Juniors and their dog show future if there were a closer continuity between the breed ring and the Junior Showmanship ring.

It is very confusing to a successful Junior handler to find that the things he was judged upon that were so important in Junior Showmanship are almost totally disregarded in the breed ring. Some of these are: eye contact, courtesy turn, not letting the judge move behind you, and changing hands both in the patterns and going around the ring. There should be a definite standard of excellence in Junior Showmanship that can be easily transferred to the breed ring. The Junior Showmanship handler of today is the successful breeder, handler, or judge of tomorrow.

Boys and girls who are over eight years old but under seventeen years of age are eligible to compete in Junior Showmanship. The following categories are most generally used for the division of classes:

Novice A Division: For boys and girls who are at least eight years old and under thirteen years old on the day of the show and who, at the time entries close, have never won in Junior Showmanship competition.

Novice B Division: For boys and girls who are at least thirteen years old and under seventeen years old on the day of the show and who, at the time entries close, have never won in Junior Showmanship competition.

Graduate Novice Division: For boys and girls who are at least eight years old and under thirteen years old on the day of the show and who, at the time entries close, have won in Junior Showmanship competition one or more times.

Open Division: For boys and girls who are at least ten years old and under seventeen years old on the day of the show and who, at the time entries close, have won in Junior Showmanship competition one or more times.

Each dog handled in a regular Junior Showmanship Class must be entered and shown in one of the Breed or Obedience Classes at the show, or must be entered for Junior Showmanship only. Each dog must be owned or co-owned by the Junior handler or by the Junior handler's father, mother, brother, sister, uncle, aunt, grandfather, or grandmother, including step and half relations. Every dog entered for Junior Showmanship must be eligible to compete in dog shows or in obedience trials. A dog that has been excused or disqualified by a breed judge or by a bench show committee may still be handled in Junior Showmanship if eligible to compete in obedience trials. A dog that has been rejected, dismissed, or excused by the veterinarian for the protection of the other dogs at the show or for the protection of the dog excused may not be handled in Junior Showmanship.

To enter Junior Showmanship competition at point shows, a section is provided on the back of each Official American Kennel Club Entry Form.

Permission to reprint this portion of the form has been granted by The American Kennel Cub.

To force feed your dog, prepare his regular food and shape the food into small egg-shaped balls.

Place the left hand on the lower jaw and pick up a ball of food with the right hand.

12
Nutrition and Feeding of Your Show Dog

Dogs are known to require at least forty-three basic nutrients in order to maintain good health. Your show dog should be fed a balanced diet. This diet must contain the correct balance of protein, carbohydrates, fats, vitamins, and minerals. It is a fact that a dog being fed a well-balanced diet, one supplying all the nutrients needed for growth and maintenance of body tissue, will be healthier and more resistant to disease than a dog receiving an inadequate diet. Good nutrition is vital to your show dog.

Commercial dog food is available in several forms—dry, semi-moist, and canned. Dry meal mixed with a canned or semi-moist product is presently considered the ideal combination for daily feeding. Manufacturers of dog food state that their products provide one hundred percent complete nutrition. However, some dog food products simply supply the *minimum* daily requirements. To offset the stress element present in the daily lives of many show dogs, a vitamin-mineral supplement is recommended.

Many dry dog foods tend to be low in fats because the fat may turn rancid if higher than a certain percentage. If you feed dry meal only, you may want to add a skin and coat conditioner to the daily diet to prevent fatty acid deficiency. A fatty acid deficiency results in dry, flaky skin and dull coat, and is often accompanied by itching and scratching. There are both oil supplements and dry mix supplements which can be added to the daily diet to help correct this problem.

Adult dogs should be fed one time per day. In the case of an underweight dog, puppy, or finicky eater, two meals are usually more suitable. Feed the dog in a quiet, confined area. To avoid digestive problems, it is a good practice to withhold water and strenuous exercise one hour before and one hour after each meal.

Once you have determined the food supplements necessary for your dog's diet, try not to change them. Generally a dog's appetite and weight are less likely to change if the dog is kept on a regular diet.

FORCE FEEDING

No matter how well balanced the nutrients in the diet may be, the diet is inadequate if the dog refuses to eat. After having your veterinarian rule out any medical reasons that may be causing the animal to refuse to eat, it may become necessary to force feed your dog to keep him from losing weight. When force feeding, take his regular food and form it into small, egg-shaped balls. Now with the left hand on the lower jaw, bracing the dog, open the dog's mouth, then take one ball in the right hand, dip it in lukewarm water, and slide it down the dog's throat. Release the hold on the jaws and close them. Stroke the dog's throat and keep his mouth closed until he swallows. Continue repeating this process until the entire meal is gone.

Remember, never add vitamins, minerals, or fatty acid supplements in excess. Over-supplementing your dog's diet can cause problems.

Dip the food ball quickly into a bowl of lukewarm water.

Open the jaws and place a food ball far back in the mouth.

Make certain you place the food ball back far enough in the mouth so that it slides easily down the throat.

Close the mouth and make sure the food ball has been swallowed. Repeat this entire procedure until the whole meal has been consumed.

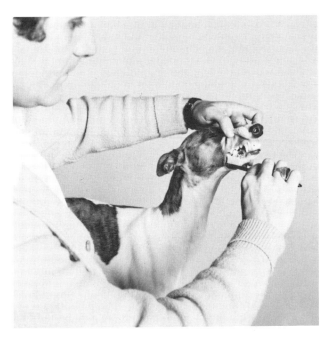
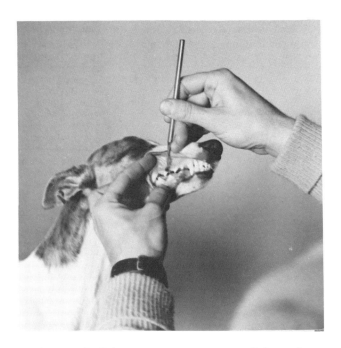

Weekly cleaning of the teeth with a toothbrush and baking soda or a dentifrice formulated for dogs is a necessary part of a good dental hygiene program. Start cleaning your dog's teeth at an early age so he will grow up accepting dental care.

If tartar builds up, you can remove it by using a dental tool. Any build-up on your dog's teeth should be removed. Always move the scraper away from the gumline.

Providing a large paddock area is an ideal way to make sure that a dog will get adequate exercise. Putting compatible dogs together in the same paddock area often encourages more running and playing and results in the dog getting more exercise.

13

Healthcare and Conditioning of Your Show Dog

Healthcare and conditioning programs for your show dog will be conducted entirely outside the show ring. However, the success of these programs pays for itself many times over when your dog is in the ring. Often a better representative of a breed that is in poor condition will place behind a lesser dog in good condtion. Remember, good overall health conditioning, or lack of them, affect your dog's chances of winning. The most important things to be worked on during conditioning are coat, weight, muscle development and muscle tone.

General guidelines for healthcare and conditioning apply to all breeds, regardless of size or age. But due to wide differences among breeds, programs must be tailored to each specific dog. It is of importance to know that the rewards of good conditioning may not become immediately apparent. Results should begin to show in four to six weeks in most dogs, and by ten weeks your dog should be well-conditioned. Consistent programs of planned conditioning and healthcare applied systematically, will be necessary to produce a top-conditioned animal. If there is no consistency in your daily care programs, there will be little benefit to your dog. Your show dog will need both external and internal conditioning, for each will affect the other.

The remainder of this chapter will be devoted to many parts of effective programs. You are probably already doing many of the things needed to build up and condi-

tion a show dog. After reading through this chapter, determine what you are doing and then make sure that all aspects of care discussed here are included in your conditioning program.

CARE OF THE EYES, EARS, AND MOUTH

To care for the eyes, ears, and mouth it is important to observe them daily. Ear problems occur more frequently in flop-eared breeds and breeds with a heavy hair growth inside the ear canal. All breeds of dogs may have ear inflammation. Some symptoms of ear problems are pawing or scratching about the ears and shaking the head, accumulation of wax in the ear, and a dark, foul smelling discharge from the ear or swelling around the ear flap. Ear inflammation is painful to the dog and may cause irritable behavior. If the condition is neglected it can be harmful to the dog's general health.

The ear canal is funnel shaped with a turn in the deepest part leading to the eardrum. Due to this shape, any accumulation that builds up can be only partially loosened by the dog's shaking his head. Flop-eared or hairy-eared breeds may be further troubled by lack of air circulation in the ear canal. This creates a condition that encourages the growth of bacteria. Breeds with long coats and flop-ears should have the hair in the ear removed every three to six weeks.

A variety of products are available for the treatment and control of ear problems such as ear cankers, ear mites, excessive wax accumulation, itching, and irritation. It is not always possible to prevent these conditions from developing. Regular examination of the ear will alert you to the start of troublesome conditions. Remember if any of these conditions persists, consult your veterinarian.

Regular inspections of your dog's eyes are extremely important to prevent minor irritations which can lead to serious problems. All breeds require regular eye care to keep eyes healthy. Some of the short-faced breeds have large round eyes set in shallow sockets. This makes them prone to eye injury or irritation.

Any discharge or accumulation at the inside cover of the eyes should be removed immediately in a sanitary manner using a cotton ball. On breeds with excessive facial hair, keeping hair away from the eyes will prevent problems from occurring. Treatment and prescription products are available for cleansing the eyes and relieving irritation.

Unfortunately, mouth and dental care are among the most neglected healthcare areas. A dog must be trained to accept dental care at an early age. To protect your dog's teeth and mouth properly, you must follow a dental hygiene program. The most common mouth problem is the build up of tartar around the gumlines. Tartar is formed by a chemical activity between the dog's saliva and food. If allowed to build up, tartar can cause gum inflammation and infection, and can result in loss of teeth. To care for your show dog, you must reduce the tartar by a weekly brushing of the teeth with a toothbrush and baking soda or a dentifrice formulated for dogs. Providing a rawhide bone and hard biscuits will also prove beneficial for jaw exercise and gum massage. When a puppy is teething, bone chewing helps to loosen baby teeth, aids in jaw development, and relieves the irritation of swollen gums.

INTERNAL PARASITES

Internal parasites, usually referred to as worms, are common in dogs. When worms go unnoticed, the dog's health may become endangered. Worm infestation is a major problem and must be controlled in order to maintain your dog's condition.

There are five types of worms: roundworms, hookworms, tapeworms, whipworms, and heartworms. The first four can be detected by your veterinarian upon examination of a fresh stool sample. Many people believe that the presence of worms in a dog can be detected by looking at stools without the aid of a microscope. This is correct only in the case of roundworms and tapeworms. The only sure policy is to provide your veterinarian with a fresh stool sample at least every six months.

Roundworms are white and are from four to seven inches long when mature. These worms swim free in the intestines. A generally poor appearance, loss of appetite and coat luster, intermittent diarrhea, and an occasional worm seen in the stools are the ususal symptoms of roundworm. *Hookworms* are white and thread-like with a hook-like appendage at one end. They live in the dog's intestines and maintain themselves by sucking blood from the wall of the animal's intestines. *Tapeworms* are white, flat, and segmented and can be over two feet long inside the intestines. The segments are one-fourth inch to inch long and can be from one-sixteenth inch to one-half inch wide. Each segment has a life of its own and can break off and pass out through the stool. Some of the symptoms are poor appearance, accompanied by a lusterless coat, mild diarrhea, and irregular appetite. *Whipworms* are small thread-like worms which live in the folds of the intestines. Symptoms are usually poor appetite and soft stools, with blood often present in the stool.

All of these types of worms can be transmitted from one dog to another. Keeping the areas your dog frequents clean, disinfected, and free of fleas can help reduce the possibility of worm infestation. Your veterinarian should be consulted for the diagnosis, treatment, and control of worms.

Heartworm infestation is an altogether different problem. Because the treatment for heartworm is sometimes fatal, prevention is essential. Your veterinarian can check for the presence of heartworm by making a bloodtest. Preventive medication for heartworm can be prescribed. Blood tests are necessary for all dogs when medication for heartworm has been stopped and when you are planning to start it again.

EXTERNAL PARASITES

Fleas and ticks are the most common external parasites and can infest your dog at any time of the year. Fleas and ticks can be a serious health problem to your dog. If neglected, your dog can become seriously ill if heavy infestation occurs.

One serious problem with infestation is that fleas bite the animal's skin. Flea bites can be extremely irritating and dogs often develop allergies which result in itching. The animal bites and scratches itself with the result that hot spots (moist eczema) or a non-specific type of dermatitis. Fleas are also the main source of tapeworm in dogs.

Products to control fleas or ticks on your dog include collars, sprays, shampoos, and dips. While easily seen on smooth-coated breeds, fleas can bury themselves in the hair of long-coated dogs. They seldom stay in one place very long and their jumping talents make killing them difficult.

Two tick species infest dogs. They are the brown dog tick, the most common variety, and the American dog tick. The brown dog tick seldom bites humans and carries no disease. The American dog tick may carry Rocky Mountain spotted fever and will bite humans. Animals pick up ticks from infested woods, fields, damp areas, and sandy beaches. Ticks attach themselves to the pet's skin and feed on its blood. Tick bites are painful and irritating to animals. The irritation leads to persistent scratching and secondary skin infections often result.

Flea collars are effective on most breeds of dogs because they contain vaporizing agents that kill fleas and aid in tick control for several months. Certain breeds may experience reactions to flea collars, so check frequently to see if this is occurring.

Before putting on a flea collar, bathing your dog with a flea shampoo will help kill fleas and ticks. There are several brands of non-irritating shampoos formulated specifically to rid dogs of fleas and ticks.

Another way to control these external parasites, prior to putting a collar on the dog, is to use a powder or spray. These are particularly effective around the hindquarters of large dogs.

EXERCISE

Exercise is vital for the general health and muscle development of your dog. The right form of exercise is extremely important to the correct development of your breed. The required exercise to build and maintain proper muscle tone and development will vary in accordance with the type and size of the breed. For example, exercise requirements for proper muscle development of a Doberman Pinscher would differ from those of a Toy Poodle.

There are several ways to ensure that your dog is obtaining sufficient exercise: first, a daily walk; second, long paddock areas where the dog can exercise freely and develop good muscle tone; third, for an intensive exercise program a bicycle can be used with the dog moving on a lead beside the bicycle, never exceeding the speed used to move the dog in the show ring. Do not allow the dog to gallop or otherwise break stride.

For the medium and larger breeds, begin your exercise program at one-half mile per day and increase the distance covered by one-half mile increments every two weeks until you have worked up to two miles per day. Care should be taken not to plan the exercise time around meals or during the heat of the day.

BEST DOG
IN
SHOW

14

Making an Entry

The official entry form necessary for American Kennel Club (AKC) point shows is simple to complete, but must be one hundred percent accurate! Entries are mailed to the show superintendent who is organizing and operating the show for a particular specialty or all-breed club. Annually, these superintendents are licensed by the AKC. A published list of upcoming shows is available in the *AKC Gazette*, in many breed magazines or premium lists, and also may be obtained by writing the AKC show department or the respective superintendents. However, some show-giving clubs do not make use of AKC licensed superintendents, electing instead to put on their own show, and these should be contacted directly. Premium lists are mailed out nationwide to individuals who have previously entered shows or who request to be on the mailing lists.

Entries must be mailed with the proper entry fee as shown on the premium list and must arrive at the superintendent's office by the listed closing date. Entries should be made *immediately* after show information becomes available *if* the show has a limited entry. Limited entry means that after the maximum number of designed entries is received, no more are accepted, regardless of closing date. Any "out of the ordinary" requirements are also listed in the premium list, *AKC Gazette*, and in some breed publications. that is why it is important to read the premium list and make sure you comply with every detail including requirements for a limited entry and different requirements within your breed such as for color.

An entry form must be signed on the front side at the bottom, and must have the AKC rules printed on the back to make it an official form. Information to be filled in on the forms should be typewritten or clearly printed in ink for protection against changes or forgery. Prior to mailing your entry, carefully check over your AKC registration to verify that all information has been transferred correctly to the entry form. Entries generally close three weeks prior to show date but the closing date is always included on the premium list.

The following is a description for each part of the Official American Kennel Club Entry Form, what it means, and what information is required for each part of the form:

1. KENNEL CLUB NAME AND DATE OF SHOW: In this area the name of the kennel club holding the show and the date of the show should be supplied. If using a blank form or a form from a previous show, write this information in yourself.

2. FEE: Obtain the fee requirement from the premium list or the *American Kennel Gazette*. If you are unable to learn the exact fee, send $10.00, and you will be notified of any remaining amount you must pay or of any refund due you.

3. BREED: Enter in this space the breed of dog you will be exhibiting at the show.

4. VARIETY: This applies to any of the breeds that are subdivided into two or more varieties.

5. DOG SHOW CLASS: In this space write the name of the regular class in which you wish to enter your dog. If your dog is an AKC champion and you wish to exhibit him in breed competition, also enter that information here.

7. CLASS DIVISION: If the dog show class in which you are entering your dog is divided, then, in addition to designating the class, specify the particular division—i.e., age division, color division, weight division.

8. ADDITIONAL CLASSES: Any additional classes you wish to enter should be written in here. Usually this will be Sweepstakes, Stud Dog Class, Brood Bitch Class, or Veterans Class.

9. OBEDIENCE TRIAL CLASS: This is to be filled in only if you are entering your dog in obedience competition. If you are not, leave this space blank.

10 & 11. JUNIOR SHOWMANSHIP: Box 10 is to be filled in only if the dog is to be handled in Junior Showmanship competition. If the dog is entered in other competition also, be sure all previous blanks are completed. In Box 11, fill in the name of the Junior handler, and be sure to fill in the Junior Showmanship section on the back of the form.

12. AKC REGISTRATION NO., ETC.: Enter the number from the dog's official registration certificate and indicate whether this is the dog's individual AKC registration number. If the individual registration number has not yet been assigned, then enter the litter number. *ILP* means Indefinite Listing Privilege and refers to dogs being entered in the Miscellaneous Class. *Foreign Registration No. & Country* applies only to imports not registered yet with the AKC. In this space be sure to check the appropriate box as well as to enter the number.

14. DATE OF BIRTH: Copy this date from the AKC registration certificate.

15. PLACE OF BIRTH: Check the appropriate box for place of birth.

16. BREEDER: The breeder of record is listed on the AKC registration certificate. The correct name should be entered here.

17. SIRE: Write in the name of the sire of the dog, as recorded on the registration certificate.

18. DAM: Write in the name of the dam of the dog, as recorded on the registration certificate.

19. ACTUAL OWNER(S): List the complete name and address of the owner(s). It is of great importance that the information entered in this section be accurate. If a dog has changed owners but the transfer application has not been processed and returned by the AKC, write "transfer applied for" after the name of the new owner.

20. NAME OF OWNER'S AGENT (IF ANY) AT THE SHOW: If applicable, write in the name of the handler who will be exhibiting your dog.

21. SIGNATURE: The owner of the dog or an authorized agent must sign the entry form. Unsigned entry forms *will not* be accepted.

OFFICIAL AMERICAN KENNEL CLUB
ENTRY FORM

☐1

☐2

NOTICE: PLEASE PUT BREED & NAME OF SHOW ON CHECK.   I ENCLOSE $ _____ for entry fees.

OFFICE USE ONLY		SC			Bd			S
CL 1	CL 2		OB 1	OB 2	JS			O

IMPORTANT — Read carefully instructions on Reverse Side Before Filling Out. Numbers in the boxes indicate sections of the instructions relevant to the information needed in that box. (PLEASE PRINT)

☐3 BREED	☐4 VARIETY	☐5 SEX

☐6 DOG SHOW CLASS	☐7 CLASS DIVISION Weight, color, etc.

☐8 ADDITIONAL CLASSES	☐9 OBEDIENCE TRIAL CLASS	☐10 JR. SHOWMANSHIP CLASS

☐11 NAME OF (see back) JUNIOR HANDLER (if any)

☐12 FULL NAME OF DOG

☐13 ☐ AKC REG NO Enter number here ☐ AKC LITTER NO ☐ I.L.P. NO. ☐ FOREIGN REG. NO. & COUNTRY	☐14 DATE OF BIRTH
	☐15 PLACE OF BIRTH ☐ U.S.A. ☐ Canada ☐ Foreign Do not print the above in catalog.

☐16 BREEDER

☐17 SIRE

☐18 DAM

☐19 ACTUAL OWNER(S)

OWNER'S ADDRESS   (PLEASE PRINT)

CITY	STATE	ZIP

☐20 NAME OF OWNER'S AGENT (IF ANY) AT THE SHOW   CODE #

☐21 I CERTIFY that I am the actual owner of the dog, or that I am the duly authorized agent of the actual owner whose name I have entered above. In considertion of the acceptance of this entry. I (we) agree to abide by the rules and regulations of The American Kennel Club in effect at the time of this show or obedience trial, and by any additional rules and regulations appearing in the premium list for this show or obedience trial or both, and further agree to be bound by the "Agreement" printed on the reverse side of this entry form. I (we) certify and represent that the dog entered is not a hazard to persons or other dogs. This entry is submitted for acceptance on the foregoing representation and agreement.

SIGNATURE of owner or his agent
duly authorized to make this entry _____

DOG SHOW JUDGING PROCEDURE

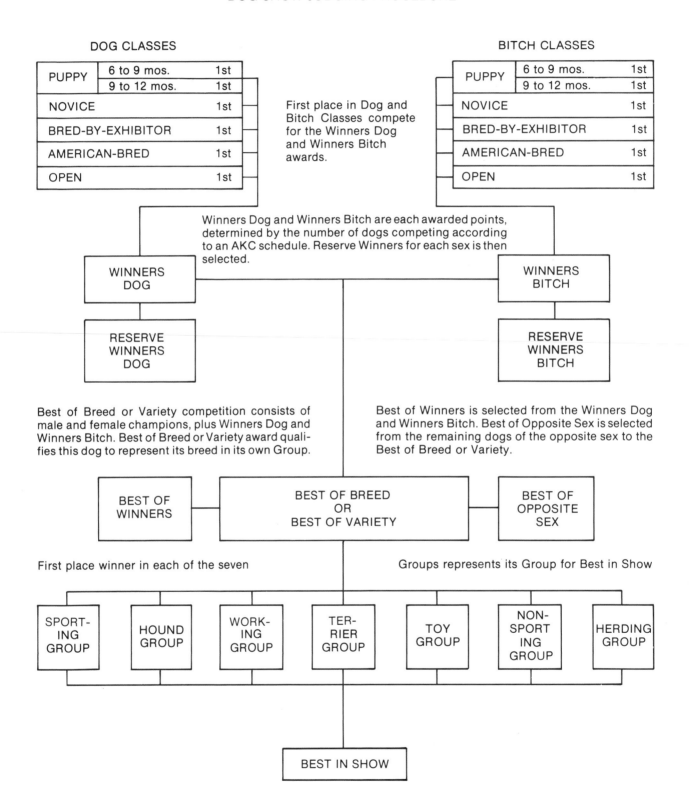

DOG CLASSES

PUPPY	6 to 9 mos.	1st
	9 to 12 mos.	1st
NOVICE		1st
BRED-BY-EXHIBITOR		1st
AMERICAN-BRED		1st
OPEN		1st

BITCH CLASSES

PUPPY	6 to 9 mos.	1st
	9 to 12 mos.	1st
NOVICE		1st
BRED-BY-EXHIBITOR		1st
AMERICAN-BRED		1st
OPEN		1st

First place in Dog and Bitch Classes compete for the Winners Dog and Winners Bitch awards.

Winners Dog and Winners Bitch are each awarded points, determined by the number of dogs competing according to an AKC schedule. Reserve Winners for each sex is then selected.

WINNERS DOG

WINNERS BITCH

RESERVE WINNERS DOG

RESERVE WINNERS BITCH

Best of Breed or Variety competition consists of male and female champions, plus Winners Dog and Winners Bitch. Best of Breed or Variety award qualifies this dog to represent its breed in its own Group.

Best of Winners is selected from the Winners Dog and Winners Bitch. Best of Opposite Sex is selected from the remaining dogs of the opposite sex to the Best of Breed or Variety.

BEST OF WINNERS

BEST OF BREED OR BEST OF VARIETY

BEST OF OPPOSITE SEX

First place winner in each of the seven   Groups represents its Group for Best in Show

SPORT-ING GROUP

HOUND GROUP

WORK-ING GROUP

TER-RIER GROUP

TOY GROUP

NON-SPORT-ING GROUP

HERDING GROUP

BEST IN SHOW

15
How Dogs Are Judged

Following is a description of the order in which dogs are judged:

CLASSES

In every breed dogs are judged first, then bitches.

Puppy—for dogs between six months and one year of age.

Novice—for dogs which have not won three first prizes in the Novice Class, a first prize in Bred-by-Exhibitor, American-bred, or Open Classes, nor **one** or more points toward their championships.

Bred-by-Exhibitor—for dogs whelped in the United States of America, or, if individually registered in The American Kennel Club Stud Book, for dogs whelped in Canada, that are six months of age and over, that are not champions, and that are owned wholly or in part by the person or by the spouse of the person who was the breeder or one of the breeders of record.

American-bred—for all dogs (except champions) six months of age and over, whelped in the United States of American, by reason of a mating which took place in the United State of America.

Open—for all dogs, American-bred or foreign-bred, six months of age or over, except in a member specialty club show held only for American-bred dogs, in which case the Open Class shall be for American-bred dogs only.

The most experienced show dogs are shown in the American-bred and Open Classes.

WINNERS

For this class the first prize winners of the above classes compete. Two awards are made—Winners and Reserve Winners.

BEST OF BREED

Dogs of either sex which are already champions and the Winners Dog and Winners Bitch compete here. One is chosen Best of Breed. This dog competes later in the Group as the representative of its breed.

BEST OF WINNERS

The Winners Dog and Winners Bitch compete in this class. One is chosen Best of Winners.

BEST OF OPPOSITE SEX

Best of Opposite Sex is selected by the judge as the best entry of the sex opposite that of the Best of Breed winner.

WHAT MAKES A CHAMPION

Championship points can be won by one dog and one bitch in each breed entered in the show. The Winners Dog and Winners Bitch receive these points. The number of points each wins at a particular show depends on the number of each sex competing in the breed. When a dog has won fifteen points, including points at two major shows, the dog becomes a champion and holds the title all of its life.

HOW A JUDGE JUDGES

As a judge sees each dog in the ring, he compares the dog to a mental picture of the perfect dog of that breed. He judges each dog on:

    Physical structure
    Gait
    Temperament
    Condition

AT THE END OF THE SHOW

The competition becomes keener and more exciting as the judging in a dog show progresses. When all breeds have been judged, one dog in each breed remains undefeated—the one which was chosen Best of Breed. These dogs are called to compete in one of the seven Groups—Sporting, Hound, Working, Terrier, Toy, Non-Sporting, or Herding. One is chosen from each Group.

The seven Group winners then meet for the final competition.

BEST IN SHOW

This is the one judged the best dog present at the show that day.

16
The American Kennel Club

The American Kennel Club (AKC) is a multi-faceted organization dedicated to the advancement of purebred dogs. An questions you might have pertaining to registering a dog, registering a litter, show entries, general rules and regulations pertaining to dog shows, matches, obedience trials, and records in general should be directed to the AKC at the following address:

> The American Kennel Club
> 51 Madison Avenue
> New York, New York 10010

The *Rules Applying to Regulations and Dog Shows* concerning point shows are important for both the novice and experienced dog exhibitors to know. By being knowledgeable of these rules and regulations you can also utilize them in relation to show activities, and educate yourself as to the constraints and requirements of the AKC pertaining to your dog, kennel, show objectives, Junior Showmanship, and more.

In general, there are four departments toward which you should direct your correspondence and questions:

1. Show Plans Department

2. Registration Department

3. Foreign Department

4. Pure-Bred Dogs—*American Kennel Gazette*

The AKC has pamphlets on all subjects ranging from general rules and regulations to how to organize and run an AKC sanctioned match. Finally, there is a library in the headquarters building in New York City housing more than ten thousand books and periodicals, a major art exhibition and collection, and an extensive photographic file dating back to the early 1900s.

For a general overview of The American Kennel Club, its functions, and its people, write the AKC for a reprint of the article entitled "Inside AKC," from the *Gazette*, September 1973, Vol. 90. No. 9.

Anatomy of a Dog

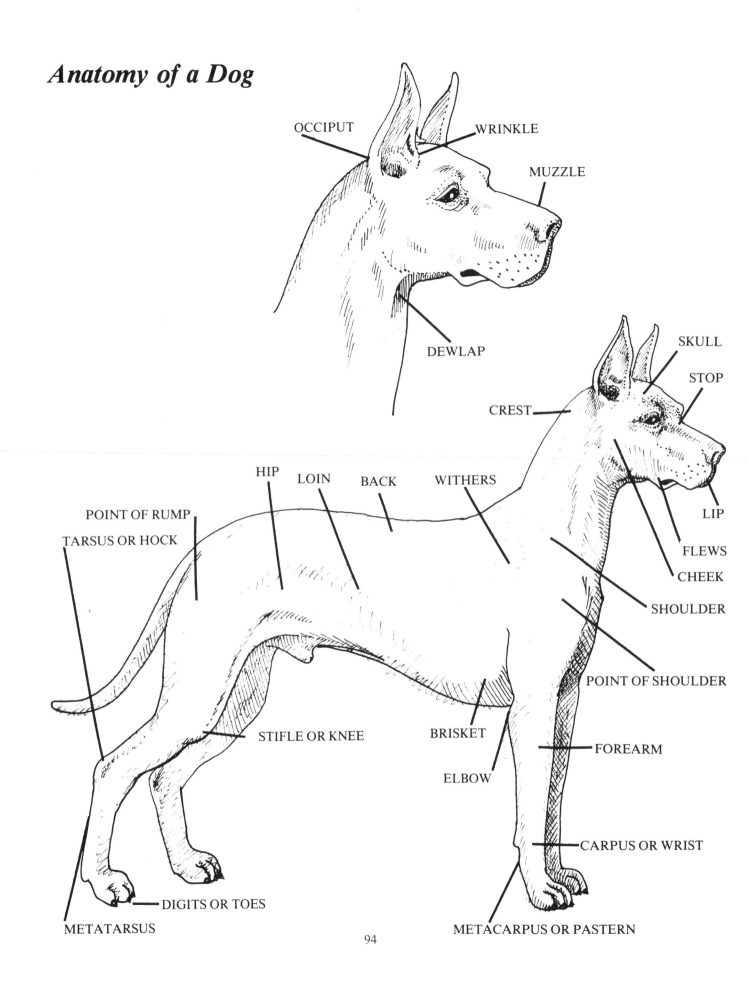

OCCIPUT

WRINKLE

MUZZLE

DEWLAP

SKULL

STOP

CREST

LIP

FLEWS

CHEEK

SHOULDER

POINT OF SHOULDER

HIP LOIN BACK WITHERS

POINT OF RUMP

TARSUS OR HOCK

STIFLE OR KNEE

BRISKET

ELBOW

FOREARM

CARPUS OR WRIST

DIGITS OR TOES

METATARSUS

METACARPUS OR PASTERN

AKC—American Kennel Club

Angulation—angle formed where the bones meet at shoulder, hip, stifle, and hock joints.

Apron—longer hair on the dog's chest

Armband—piece of paper, with the number of your entry printed on it, worn on your left upper arm

Back—area on a dog between the shoulder and tail

Bad mouth—incorrect mouth for a dog as specified by the breed Standard

Bait—piece of food, usually liver, used in the ring to keep the dog's attention

Bench show—dog show where dogs are "benched" in crates or stalls

Bitch—female dog

Bitchy—Refined appearing male

BIS—Best in Show, awarded to the dog judged as best of all breeds at a dog show

Bodied up—full-bodied or developed to full maturity

Bite—position of the upper and lower teeth when mouth is fully closed

Breeder—person who breeds dogs

Brisket—forward part of body below chest, between the forelegs

Buttocks—rump or rear

Canine—dog; or the two upper or lower teeth behind the incisors

Ch.—Champion: prefix used with the dog's registered name signifying he has earned the necessary number of points and has received this title from The American Kennel Club

Chest—part of the body enclosed by the ribs

Clip—method of trimming the coat of certain breeds

Close coupled—being short from withers to hipbones

Coat—hair covering the dog

Cobby—compact or short bodied

Conformation—physical make-up

Cropping—trimming of the ears

Croup—rear part of the back located around the tail

Dam—female parent or mother

Disqualification—decision made by judge or bench show committee that a dog has a condition making him ineligible for further competition under the dog show rules or under the breed Standard

Down in pastern—weak or faulty pastern

Elbow—joint between the upper arm and the forearm

Elbows out—elbows turning out from the body or not held close

Fault—feature of the dog that deviates from the Standard of the breed

Finished—having earned the necessary points for a championship title

Front—forepart of the body, including the forelegs, chest, brisket, and shoulders

Gait—the way in which a dog moves

Groom—to brush, comb, trim, or otherwise work on the appearance of a dog's coat

Hackney—high lifting of front feet

Height—measurement of the dog from the withers to the ground

Hock—area between hock joint and the foot

Judge—person in the dog show ring who ranks dogs based on the breed Standard

Knuckling over—bending over at the pastern

Loaded shoulders—over-developed shoulders

Loin—region on the body of the dog on either side of the spinal column between the last rib and the hindquarters

Muzzle—face of the dog in front of the eye

Pacing—moving the legs on the same side of the body in unison

Paddling—moving the forefeet wide

Pastern—region of the foreleg between the wrist (or carpus) and the toes

Professional handler—person who earns his living by showing dogs for their owners for a fee

Puppy—dog under the age of twelve months

Rocking horse—when dog stands so that the front and rear legs are extended out from the body

Roach back—an irregular raising of the topline over the loin area so that the back has a convex appearance

Set up—a dog that is stacked or posed by hand

Special—a champion usually competing in the Best of Breed Class

Sire—male parent or father

Stacking—posing or setting up a dog

Straight shoulders—shoulder blades are straight up and down, due to insufficient angulation

Standard—description of the "ideal" in each breed

Substance—bone

Swayback—back sagging in the middle

Trim—to remove excess hair

Tucked-up—belly well pulled up under loin

Whiskers—longer hair on sides of muzzle and underjaw